Sunday Snippets
FROM FR. DAN

**Everyday Lessons for Living
a Christ-Centered Life**

FR. DANIEL F. X. POWELL JR.

WESTBOW
PRESS®
A DIVISION OF THOMAS NELSON
& ZONDERVAN

Copyright © 2022 Fr. Daniel F. X. Powell Jr.

All rights reserved. No part of this book may be used or reproduced by any means, graphic, electronic, or mechanical, including photocopying, recording, taping or by any information storage retrieval system without the written permission of the author except in the case of brief quotations embodied in critical articles and reviews.

WestBow Press books may be ordered through booksellers or by contacting:

WestBow Press
A Division of Thomas Nelson & Zondervan
1663 Liberty Drive
Bloomington, IN 47403
www.westbowpress.com
844-714-3454

Because of the dynamic nature of the Internet, any web addresses or links contained in this book may have changed since publication and may no longer be valid. The views expressed in this work are solely those of the author and do not necessarily reflect the views of the publisher, and the publisher hereby disclaims any responsibility for them.

Any people depicted in stock imagery provided by Getty Images are models, and such images are being used for illustrative purposes only. Certain stock imagery © Getty Images.

Scripture excerpts in this work are taken from the Lectionary for Mass for Use in the Diocese of the United States of America Copyright C 2001, 19987, 1997, 1991, 1986, 1970 by the Confraternity of Christian Doctrine, Washington, D.C. Used with Permission. All Rights Reserved. No Part of the New American Bible may be reproduced in any form without permission in writing from the copyright owner.

ISBN: 978-1-6642-5429-9 (sc)
ISBN: 978-1-6642-5428-2 (hc)
ISBN: 978-1-6642-5430-5 (e)

Library of Congress Control Number: 2021925840

Print information available on the last page.

WestBow Press rev. date: 3/7/2022

To my parents, Anna and Daniel Powell, Sr.
I will be forever grateful for
your love and support

Contents

Foreword ix
Be Prepared 4
God Is Waiting 12
It's All About Me: Temptation 18
Have Faith the Size of a Mustard Seed 24
"Faith Is Trusting His Direction without
    Knowing Our Destination" 31
Sacred Scripture: Let God Talk to Your Heart 37
The Strength to Believe 44
Called by Name 51
Unmask! 58
Making Good Choices 64
Stay Awake 71
God's Time 78
God Is with Us 84
Families 90
The Face of Jesus 96
Here Am I, Lord; I Come to Do Your Will 102
The Road Less Traveled 109
Beware of the Packaging! 115
Pointed Toward the Lord 123
Invite the Lord In 131
Still and Quiet with the Lord 137
Standing in His Grace 145

Foreword

As many people of faith, I look for ways to deepen my prayer experience and apply the gospel teachings to my daily life. As a member of Fr. Dan Powell's parish church, his homilies accomplish these tasks for me regularly.

This encouraged—no, in fact, inspired—me to share some of his many relatable insights so Christians everywhere could use them as a tool to enhance their relationship with Jesus. To make Fr. Dan's homilies more enriching, I have included the Sunday readings upon which he based his reflections.

I believe that not only can this book be used as an insightful, spiritual text, but it can be a prayer guide for meditation and adoration during times of extended silent prayer. It is my hope and prayer that Fr. Dan's spiritual perspective will deepen your faith journey as it indeed has mine.

Finally, while the inspiration was mine to share the spiritual fire of Fr. Dan, my idea could never have realized its potential without the dedication and support of my friend, Angela Richards. She took my vision and helped to make it a reality in a way I doubt anyone else could. Her tireless work is a testimony to her deep faith, and I am profoundly grateful for her witness and talent.

Marcie McCarthy

READINGS FOR SEPTEMBER 1, 2019

First Reading
Sirach 3:17–18, 20, 28–29
My child, conduct your affairs with humility,
and you will be loved more than a giver of gifts.
Humble yourself the more, the greater you are,
and you will find favor with God.
What is too sublime for you, seek not,
into things beyond your strength search not.
The mind of a sage appreciates proverbs,
and an attentive ear is the joy of the wise.
Water quenches a flaming fire,
and alms atone for sins.

Responsorial Psalm
Psalm 68:4–7, 10–11
R. God, in your goodness, you have made a home for the poor.
The just rejoice and exult before God;
they are glad and rejoice.
Sing to God, chant praise to his name;
whose name is the LORD. **R.**

The father of orphans and the defender of widows
is God in his holy dwelling.
God gives a home to the forsaken;
he leads forth prisoners to prosperity. **R.**

A bountiful rain you showered down, O God, upon your inheritance;
you restored the land when it languished;
your flock settled in it;
in your goodness, O God, you provided it for the needy. **R.**

Second Reading

Hebrews 12:18–19, 22–24A

Brothers and sisters:
you have not approached that which could be touched
and a blazing fire and gloomy darkness
and storm and a trumpet blast
and a voice speaking words such that those who heard
begged that no message be further addressed to them.
No, you have approached Mount Zion
and the city of the living God, the heavenly Jerusalem,
and countless angels in festal gathering,
and the assembly of the firstborn enrolled in heaven,
and God the judge of all,
and the spirits of the just made perfect,
and Jesus, the mediator of a new covenant,
and the sprinkled blood that speaks more eloquently than that of Abel.

Gospel

Luke 14:1, 7–14

On a sabbath Jesus went to dine
at the home of one of the leading Pharisees,
and the people there were observing him carefully.

He told a parable to those who had been invited,
noticing how they were choosing the places of honor at the table.
"When you are invited by someone to a wedding banquet,
do not recline at table in the place of honor.
A more distinguished guest than you may have been invited by him,
and the host who invited both of you may approach you and say,
'Give your place to this man,'
and then you would proceed with embarrassment
to take the lowest place.
Rather, when you are invited,
go and take the lowest place
so that when the host comes to you he may say,
'My friend, move up to a higher position.'

Then you will enjoy the esteem of your companions at the table.
For every one who exalts himself will be humbled,
but the one who humbles himself will be exalted."
Then he said to the host who invited him,
"When you hold a lunch or a dinner,
do not invite your friends or your brothers
or your relatives or your wealthy neighbors,
in case they may invite you back and you have repayment.
Rather, when you hold a banquet,
invite the poor, the crippled, the lame, the blind;
blessed indeed will you be because of their inability to repay you.
For you will be repaid at the resurrection of the righteous."

Be Prepared

HOMILY GIVEN ON SEPTEMBER 1, 2019

We know that Hurricane Dorian is in the Bahamas and beginning to strike that island in the next few hours, and we know that the hurricane was forecast to hit Florida. Now it is forecast to possibly go up the coast. It is still going to cause a lot of damage and destruction wherever it goes. Hurricanes are completely out of our control. We cannot say to a hurricane, "Would you mind? Instead of here, would you mind going somewhere else? Would you mind not doing this?" We can't do that.

However, when there is a hurricane coming, people can prepare. They can take care of all the different precautions, listen to all the different warnings, and make sure they're doing everything they possibly can to ensure they know where the hurricane is going to be and relocate to the best location possible.

Hurricanes and life have a lot in common because much that happens in our lives is out of our control. We would like to control everything, but we can only control what we can because so much of life is out of our control. However, we can be prepared, and the way we prepare is simply by keeping God as a part of our life consciously every day, remembering that God is always there. When life seems like it is completely out of control, we can remember that we have something that can anchor us. We can hold onto a rock, the Rock of Jesus Christ.

Another way we prepare ourselves for life's struggles is by receiving Jesus in the Eucharist. We take His body and blood, and it goes deep within us. Then when we have times when we feel our lives are out of control, we can remember that we are as prepared as best we can because we have consciously invited the Lord Jesus Christ into our very bodies.

It is Labor Day weekend, and we remember in a special way all those workers who labor in any way. Those of us here today work in different ways. We use the gifts and talents that we have been given differently. We also remember that all the gifts and talents we have, have been given to us by God.

The readings today speak about humility. Each of us needs to be humble enough to recognize that all the gifts and talents we have ultimately come from Him and that all the gifts and talents He has given to anybody else have come from Him as well. However, we can fall into jealousy. We can fall into wishing we had the same gifts and possessions as somebody else. We must stay humble and grateful for our own gifts. Humility does not mean we beat ourselves up. Humility means we thank God for whatever He has given to us and whatever He has given to others. We trust that ultimately He is in control and we are not.

We can look at hurricanes and say, "Well, where were you God? Why would you let that happen?" God does not bring storms into our lives, but He allows them because, in His infinite wisdom, we can, and do, grow closer to Him during the storms of our lives. During those times when we are not in control, the first reading said, "My child, conduct your affairs with humility." Being humble means we recognize that ultimately we are children of God and it is okay to go before the Lord as His child and ask Him for His grace and strength. "Humble yourself the more, the greater you are, and you will find favor with God." When greater things happen to us, we do not need to say, "Oh, it was no big deal!" We need to thank God all the more! "What is too sublime for you, seek not, Into things beyond your strength, search not." **So many times, we can seek all the praise here and forget who ultimately deserves the praise.**

In the second reading, we heard, "you have approached Mount Zion and the city of the living God." What does it mean, and what does it look like if we approach the living God each day? So many times, we want to go the other way. Oftentimes we do not approach Him at all. What does it mean for us? What does it look like if we approach the Lord and come before Him? Perhaps it is as simple as, "Lord, I humbly place myself in

Your presence. I know You are here. I know You will take care of me. I know You will take care of this situation. Give me the grace to trust." It is then that we are taking the chance to approach the Lord. **Tomorrow, approach the Lord again and then the next day, but we start today. Take the chance to approach Him.**

In the gospel, people were observing Jesus carefully to make sure He knew what He was doing. He basically said that people like to take the high seat at a table because it is a place of honor. Jesus suggested taking the low seat because if we take the high seat, somebody greater might come and we will be embarrassed if we are asked to give the high seat to someone else and then have to take the low seat. I wonder what we would have done if we had been invited to that banquet? What do we do now? When we get invited to banquets, when we go to a restaurant, do we say, "That's the best seat. I'm going to take that seat"? Or do we say, "No, you take the better seat"? We have so many opportunities every day to place ourselves in a spirit of humility, and again, humility does not mean we beat ourselves up or put ourselves down. It simply means we recognize, when we put God first, that allows us to do things completely differently. "Rather, when you hold a banquet, invite the poor, the crippled, the lame, the blind." My guess is none of us are going to have a Labor Day picnic where we invite the poor, the blind, and the crippled. Maybe we could stop and see when we can incorporate somebody else into our lives, somebody in need perhaps. Is there somebody out there that we could be nicer to or we need to reach out to a little bit differently? Maybe there is somebody out there to whom we need to be a little humbler?

So we pray for all those affected by Hurricane Dorian. We pray that they will be safe. We pray to recognize the reality and to be humble enough to see that there is so much that is out of our control and that we have to be prepared. **The chief way we prepare is by letting God be a part of each day by receiving Him in the Eucharist and by allowing Him to truly dwell within us. May we take the chance today! May we approach the Lord!**

READINGS FOR SEPTEMBER 15, 2019

First Reading
Exodus 32:7–11, 13–14
The LORD said to Moses,
"Go down at once to your people,
whom you brought out of the land of Egypt,
for they have become depraved.
They have soon turned aside from the way I pointed out to them,
making for themselves a molten calf and worshiping it,
sacrificing to it and crying out,
'This is your God, O Israel,
who brought you out of the land of Egypt!'
"I see how stiff-necked this people is," continued the LORD to Moses.
"Let me alone, then,
that my wrath may blaze up against them to consume them.
Then I will make of you a great nation."
But Moses implored the LORD, his God, saying,
"Why, O LORD, should your wrath blaze up against your own people,
whom you brought out of the land of Egypt
with such great power and with so strong a hand?
Remember your servants Abraham, Isaac, and Israel,
and how you swore to them by your own self, saying,
'I will make your descendants as numerous as the stars in the sky;
and all this land that I promised,
I will give your descendants as their perpetual heritage.'"
So the LORD relented in the punishment
he had threatened to inflict on his people.

Responsorial Psalm
Psalm 51:3–4, 12–13, 17, 19
R. **I will rise and go to my father.**
Have mercy on me, O God, in your goodness;
in the greatness of your compassion wipe out my offense.
Thoroughly wash me from my guilt
and of my sin cleanse me. **R.**

A clean heart create for me, O God,
and a steadfast spirit renew within me.
Cast me not out from your presence,
and your Holy Spirit take not from me. **R.**

O Lord, open my lips,
and my mouth shall proclaim your praise.
My sacrifice, O God, is a contrite spirit;
a heart contrite and humbled, O God, you will not spurn. **R.**

Second Reading
1 Timothy 1:12–17
Beloved:
I am grateful to him who has strengthened me, Christ Jesus our Lord,
because he considered me trustworthy
in appointing me to the ministry.
I was once a blasphemer and a persecutor and arrogant,
but I have been mercifully treated
because I acted out of ignorance in my unbelief.
Indeed, the grace of our Lord has been abundant,
along with the faith and love that are in Christ Jesus.
This saying is trustworthy and deserves full acceptance:
Christ Jesus came into the world to save sinners.
Of these I am the foremost.
But for that reason I was mercifully treated,
so that in me, as the foremost,
Christ Jesus might display all his patience as an example
for those who would come to believe in him for everlasting life.
To the king of ages, incorruptible, invisible, the only God,
honor and glory, forever and ever. Amen.

Gospel
Luke 15:1–32
Tax collectors and sinners were all drawing near to listen to Jesus,
but the Pharisees and scribes began to complain, saying,
"This man welcomes sinners and eats with them."

So to them he addressed this parable.
"What man among you having a hundred sheep and losing one of them
would not leave the ninety-nine in the desert
and go after the lost one until he finds it?
And when he does find it,
he sets it on his shoulders with great joy
and, upon his arrival home,
he calls together his friends and neighbors and says to them,
'Rejoice with me because I have found my lost sheep.'
I tell you, in just the same way
there will be more joy in heaven over one sinner who repents
than over ninety-nine righteous people
who have no need of repentance.
"Or what woman having ten coins and losing one
would not light a lamp and sweep the house,
searching carefully until she finds it?
And when she does find it,
she calls together her friends and neighbors
and says to them,
'Rejoice with me because I have found the coin that I lost.'
In just the same way, I tell you,
there will be rejoicing among the angels of God
over one sinner who repents."
Then he said,
"A man had two sons, and the younger son said to his father,
'Father give me the share of your estate that should come to me.'
So the father divided the property between them.
After a few days, the younger son collected all his belongings
and set off to a distant country
where he squandered his inheritance on a life of dissipation.
When he had freely spent everything,
a severe famine struck that country,
and he found himself in dire need.
So he hired himself out to one of the local citizens
who sent him to his farm to tend the swine.
And he longed to eat his fill of the pods on which the swine fed,

but nobody gave him any.
Coming to his senses he thought,
'How many of my father's hired workers
have more than enough food to eat,
but here am I, dying from hunger.
I shall get up and go to my father and I shall say to him,
"Father, I have sinned against heaven and against you.
I no longer deserve to be called your son;
treat me as you would treat one of your hired workers."'
So he got up and went back to his father.
While he was still a long way off,
his father caught sight of him,
and was filled with compassion.
He ran to his son, embraced him and kissed him.
His son said to him,
'Father, I have sinned against heaven and against you;
I no longer deserve to be called your son.'
But his father ordered his servants,
'Quickly bring the finest robe and put it on him;
put a ring on his finger and sandals on his feet.
Take the fattened calf and slaughter it.
Then let us celebrate with a feast,
because this son of mine was dead, and has come to life again;
he was lost, and has been found.'
Then the celebration began.
Now the older son had been out in the field
and, on his way back, as he neared the house,
he heard the sound of music and dancing.
He called one of the servants and asked what this might mean.
The servant said to him,
'Your brother has returned
and your father has slaughtered the fattened calf
because he has him back safe and sound.'
He became angry,
and when he refused to enter the house,
his father came out and pleaded with him.

He said to his father in reply,
'Look, all these years I served you
and not once did I disobey your orders;
yet you never gave me even a young goat to feast on with my friends.
But when your son returns,
who swallowed up your property with prostitutes,
for him you slaughter the fattened calf.'
He said to him,
'My son, you are here with me always;
everything I have is yours.
But now we must celebrate and rejoice,
because your brother was dead and has come to life again;
he was lost and has been found.'"

God Is Waiting

HOMILY GIVEN ON SEPTEMBER 15, 2019

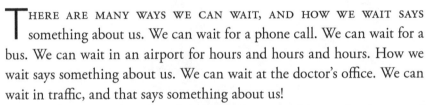

There are many ways we can wait, and how we wait says something about us. We can wait for a phone call. We can wait for a bus. We can wait in an airport for hours and hours and hours. How we wait says something about us. We can wait at the doctor's office. We can wait in traffic, and that says something about us!

In today's gospel, we heard the familiar story of the prodigal son, and in that gospel, there is a point where we are told that the father saw his son coming from a distance. To see him coming from a distance, he had to be waiting for him. It does not say he just happened to be there. There he is. But he saw him from a distance, and then he ran to him. So when he was waiting, he was hoping that somehow his son would return, that somehow his son would see that he needed to live his life differently.

Our heavenly Father does the same thing with us. He waits. He is waiting, and He wants to run to us. But He is not going to force himself on us. I wonder if something is going on in our lives right now and the Lord wants us to come to Him. The Lord wants us to walk to Him and ask for His help. He wants us to recognize that we can't do it without His help. "I cannot do this on my own, Lord!" The Lord is there waiting. All we need to do is approach Him, and He's right there to be our grace and our strength.

The gospel also tells us, "there will be rejoicing among the Angels of God over one sinner who repents." God loves each one of us, and somehow

I do not know how He does it. He pays attention to each one of us and for each one of us. **He is there with His arms outstretched ready to help us with whatever is going on in our lives. Whatever it is, we can approach Him. We can bring it to Him. He is there, waiting.**

We are told that the younger son had freely spent everything. Nobody forced him to use everything he had in a bad way. He just freely did it. Most of our decisions, if not all of them, we make freely. Usually, nobody forces us to do anything. When we include the Lord in all we are, then those freely made decisions are made with a much better foundation. This does not mean they are always going to work out the way we want them to, but freely, we can always choose to include the Lord or not.

Even while the son was still a long way off, the father in the gospel today caught sight of him and was filled with great love. He ran to his son, embraced him, and kissed him, filled with compassion for his son. **That is what the Lord is, compassionate.** Sometimes we can look at Him and think he is vengeful. No! **He is filled with compassion. He is waiting for us to come back to Him.** He is not there ready to beat us up. He is ready to embrace and kiss us. The son was lost and has been found. There are times we can feel lost, not exactly sure where we are going. What is around the corner? But the Lord wants to find us. He wants to be a part of everything. We are told the older son was angry. My guess is most of us would be angry as well. What is going on here? We are not angry when God shows us His mercy. We are not angry when someone we love or someone we have hurt shows us mercy, but sometimes we can get angry when somebody else is shown mercy. **Today, we ask God for the grace to show mercy to others as He has shown it to us, to not be angry when somebody else has been shown mercy, to not be angry when somebody else has something we think we deserve.**

The second reading tells us, "I am grateful to Him who has strengthened me." We also can be grateful that the Lord is waiting for us. He wants to strengthen us. We have been mercifully treated. All we need to do is to ask God to give us the grace to be merciful to others. Christ Jesus came into the world to save sinners. Paul claimed to be foremost a sinner, but maybe we feel like we are the worst sinner in the world too. Perhaps we feel like there is something we just cannot be forgiven for, but God, our heavenly Father, is there waiting for us. He is waiting for us to come to

Him and ask for forgiveness. If we just come to Him, He will forgive us. Thank goodness God is patient with us.

The last line of the psalm is "a heart contrite and humbled, oh God, You will not spurn." Are we humble enough to come before the Lord? Can we be humble enough to let Him into our hearts? May we be humble enough to freely go to Him and allow Him to be our strength? In the first reading, Moses implored the Lord, and then the Lord relented of the punishment. God had threatened Moses. Moses asked, and the Lord listened. The Lord does the same for us. **Sometimes we feel like He's not listening because He does not do what we want, but He is always listening.** How we wait says something about ourselves. Whether it is in an airport or traffic, He is listening. **The Lord is waiting just as the father in the prodigal son story. The Lord is waiting. He is there. May we have the courage to turn to Him! When we humble ourselves before Him, we allow Him to be our strength and hope. When we take that first step toward God, He then will run toward us.**

READINGS FOR SEPTEMBER 22, 2019

First Reading
Amos 8:4–7
Hear this, you who trample upon the needy
and destroy the poor of the land!
"When will the new moon be over," you ask,
"that we may sell our grain,
and the sabbath, that we may display the wheat?
We will diminish the ephah,
add to the shekel,
and fix our scales for cheating!
We will buy the lowly for silver,
and the poor for a pair of sandals;
even the refuse of the wheat we will sell!"
The LORD has sworn by the pride of Jacob:
Never will I forget a thing they have done!

Responsorial Psalm
Psalm 113:1–2, 4–8
R. Praise the Lord who lifts up the poor.
or:
R. Alleluia.
Praise, you servants of the LORD,
praise the name of the LORD.
Blessed be the name of the LORD
both now and forever. **R.**

High above all nations is the LORD;
above the heavens is his glory.
Who is like the LORD, our God, who is enthroned on high
and looks upon the heavens and the earth below? **R.**

He raises up the lowly from the dust;
from the dunghill he lifts up the poor
to seat them with princes,
with the princes of his own people. **R.**

Second Reading

1 Timothy 2:1–8

Beloved:

First of all, I ask that supplications, prayers,
petitions, and thanksgivings be offered for everyone,
for kings and for all in authority,
that we may lead a quiet and tranquil life
in all devotion and dignity.
This is good and pleasing to God, our savior,
who wills everyone to be saved
and to come to knowledge of the truth.
For there is one God.
There is also one mediator between God and men, the man, Christ Jesus,
who gave himself as ransom for all.
This was the testimony at the proper time.
For this I was appointed preacher and apostle
—I am speaking the truth, I am not lying—,
teacher of the Gentiles in faith and truth.
It is my wish, then, that in every place the men should pray,
lifting up holy hands, without anger or argument.

Gospel

Luke 16:1–13

Jesus said to his disciples,
"A rich man had a steward
who was reported to him for squandering his property.
He summoned him and said,
'What is this I hear about you?
Prepare a full account of your stewardship,
because you can no longer be my steward.'
The steward said to himself, 'What shall I do,
now that my master is taking the position of steward away from me?
I am not strong enough to dig and I am ashamed to beg.
I know what I shall do so that,
when I am removed from the stewardship,
they may welcome me into their homes.'

He called in his master's debtors one by one.
To the first he said,
'How much do you owe my master?'
He replied, 'One hundred measures of olive oil.'
He said to him, 'Here is your promissory note.
Sit down and quickly write one for fifty.'
Then to another the steward said, 'And you, how much do you owe?'
He replied, 'One hundred kors of wheat.'
The steward said to him, 'Here is your promissory note;
write one for eighty.'
And the master commended that dishonest steward for acting prudently.

"For the children of this world
are more prudent in dealing with their own generation
than are the children of light.
I tell you, make friends for yourselves with dishonest wealth,
so that when it fails, you will be welcomed into eternal dwellings.
The person who is trustworthy in very small matters
is also trustworthy in great ones;
and the person who is dishonest in very small matters
is also dishonest in great ones.
If, therefore, you are not trustworthy with dishonest wealth,
who will trust you with true wealth?
If you are not trustworthy with what belongs to another,
who will give you what is yours?
No servant can serve two masters.
He will either hate one and love the other,
or be devoted to one and despise the other.
You cannot serve both God and mammon."

It's All About Me: Temptation

HOMILY GIVEN ON SEPTEMBER 22, 2019

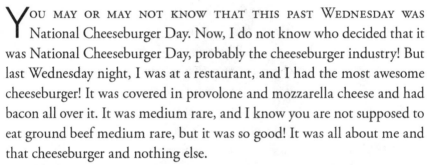

You may or may not know that this past Wednesday was National Cheeseburger Day. Now, I do not know who decided that it was National Cheeseburger Day, probably the cheeseburger industry! But last Wednesday night, I was at a restaurant, and I had the most awesome cheeseburger! It was covered in provolone and mozzarella cheese and had bacon all over it. It was medium rare, and I know you are not supposed to eat ground beef medium rare, but it was so good! It was all about me and that cheeseburger and nothing else.

The first part of the gospel tonight is all about the steward and nobody else. It was all about him. The steward complained because he was about to lose his job and he was concerned that he was going to have to go out and beg for money. So he decided he was going to take care of himself by cheating his master. He was going to make sure all his needs were satisfied! Then what is the master to do? "the master commended that dishonest steward for acting prudently." You see, the master too was focused on this world.

The reading talked about dishonest wealth. We can use a different word for "dishonest." We can use the word "worldly" wealth. What Jesus basically questioned was how we use our worldly wealth; the steward used it for his own gain. Then Jesus wants to know how the steward will use his master's resources. And the steward used his master's resources to benefit himself. It was all about him. But Jesus tells us that we need to use our Master's resources to help others!

Some of us are very charitable. A few of us are very giving. Most of us, I think, look for opportunities to help others in need. A few weeks ago, I spoke about whether we focus on ourselves or the Lord. When we focus on the Lord, He can work through us and do amazing things. Sometimes those who are dishonest, those who are only thinking about themselves, are better at doing that than those of us who are trying to do God's will in our lives. **"No servant can serve two masters. He will either hate one and love the other, or be devoted to one and despise the other. You cannot serve both God and mammon."**

I wonder how many times a day we can choose whether we are going to serve God or not, whether we are going to serve man, or whether we are going to serve ourselves. Yes, we need to take care of ourselves. Yes, we need to do certain things. But in the end, Jesus is asking us to take care of all of God's people. How do we do that? We have our Bridges Community here with us tonight, people with disabilities. How can we help people with disabilities? Who might God be asking me to reach out to, to show His face to, and to give a helping hand to? Maybe we are resisting.

We all know that we are supposed to serve God and not man. It is just there are so many temptations to serve man, so many temptations to say, "It's all about me." While I was eating that cheeseburger, it was all about me and that cheeseburger! Sometimes it is about us. But **tonight we simply ask God for the grace to make it about Him, to make it all about Him!**

The last line of the second reading said, "It is my wish, then, that in every place the men should pray, lifting up holy hands, without anger or argument." I wonder if we can even go a day without anger or argument. If we could, wouldn't that be wonderful? Things are going to come up. Things are going to happen. Serious things are going to happen. But how do we deal with them? If I am focusing on myself and it is all about me, I am going to deal with them one way. If I am focusing on the Lord and it is all about Him, I am going to deal with them differently. When we leave this church after receiving Our Lord in the Eucharist and we truly have allowed Him to enter deep within us, then we are going to focus on Him.

In the second reading, St. Paul said, "I asked that supplications, prayers and petitions and thanksgivings be offered for everyone, for kings and for all in authority, for everyone." They probably did not want to pray for kings or people in authority. We probably do not want to pray for kings or people in authority. We probably all have people we do not want to pray for. How do we serve the Lord? By praying for people we might not want to pray for or by helping someone we might not really want to help! "This is good and pleasing to God, our Savior, who wills everyone to be saved and to come to knowledge of the truth." **The Lord wills everyone to be saved. He wants each one of us to share in that great gift of eternal life. But again, He is not going to force us.**

In the first reading, we heard, "'When will the new moon be over, you ask?'" In other words, when are we going to be done with this religious stuff so I can go on with the rest of my life? This might be what we are saying tonight. "When is this Mass going to be over so I can get on with the rest of my life?" But the Lord reminds us that what happens we take with us. Then the first reading goes on to mention the idea of cheating the poor, "display the wheat? We will diminish the ephah, add to the shekel, and fix our scales for cheating!"

The psalm then goes on to say, "Praise the Lord who lifts up the poor." The psalm is saying those in need should be lifted up. Sometimes it is hard for it not to be all about us. On Wednesday night, it was all about me and that cheeseburger, and it was so good! We all have those moments that could be all about us. **But tonight, we pray for the grace to let it be about Jesus. When it is all about Him, then He'll guide us and lead us to what we need to do here, what we need to do for ourselves, and what we need to do for others.**

READINGS FOR OCTOBER 6, 2019

First Reading
Habakkuk 1:2–3; 2:2–4
How long, O LORD? I cry for help
But you do not listen!
I cry out to you, "Violence!"
But you do not intervene.
Why do you let me see ruin;
Why must I look at misery?
Destruction and violence are before me;
there is strife, and clamorous discord.
Then the LORD answered me and said:
Write down the vision clearly upon the tablets,
so that one can read it readily.
For the vision still has its time,
presses on to fulfillment, and will not disappoint;
if it delays, wait for it,
it will surely come, it will not be late.
The rash one has no integrity;
but the just one, because of his faith, shall live.

Responsorial Psalm
Psalm 95:1–2, 6–9
R. If today you hear his voice, harden not your hearts.
Come, let us sing joyfully to the Lord;
let us acclaim the Rock of our salvation.
Let us come into his presence with thanksgiving;
Let us joyfully sing psalms to him. **R.**

Come, let us bow down in worship;
let us kneel before the LORD who made us.
For he is our God,
and we are the people he shepherds, the flock he guides. **R.**

Oh, that today you would hear his voice:
"Harden not your hearts as at Meribah,
as in the day of Massah in the desert,
where your fathers tempted me;
they tested me though they had seen my works." **R.**

Second Reading
2 Timothy 1:6–8, 13–14
Beloved:
I remind you to stir into flame
the gift of God that you have through the imposition of my hands.
For God did not give us a spirit of cowardice
but rather of power and love and self-control.
So do not be ashamed of your testimony to our Lord,
nor of me, a prisoner for his sake;
but bear your share of hardship for the gospel
with the strength that comes from God.

Take as your norm the sound words that you heard from me,
in the faith and love that are in Christ Jesus.
Guard this rich trust with the help of the Holy Spirit
that dwells within us.

Gospel
Luke 17:5–10
The apostles said to the Lord, "Increase our faith."
The Lord replied,
"If you have faith the size of a mustard seed,
you would say to this mulberry tree,
'Be uprooted and planted in the sea,' and it would obey you.

"Who among you would say to your servant
who has just come in from plowing or tending sheep in the field,
'Come here immediately and take your place at table'?
Would he not rather say to him,
'Prepare something for me to eat.

Put on your apron and wait on me while I eat and drink.
You may eat and drink when I am finished'?
Is he grateful to that servant because he did what was commanded?
So should it be with you.
When you have done all you have been commanded,
say, 'We are unprofitable servants;
we have done what we were obliged to do.'"

Have Faith the Size of a Mustard Seed

HOMILY GIVEN ON OCTOBER 6, 2019

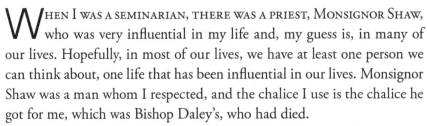

When I was a seminarian, there was a priest, Monsignor Shaw, who was very influential in my life and, my guess is, in many of our lives. Hopefully, in most of our lives, we have at least one person we can think about, one life that has been influential in our lives. Monsignor Shaw was a man whom I respected, and the chalice I use is the chalice he got for me, which was Bishop Daley's, who had died.

When he gave me this chalice, he put three of them on the table and asked, "Which one do you like?"

I may have told this story before, but it is worth telling again. One was amazingly simple, one was middle of the road, and one was ornate.

I didn't know what answer he wanted me to give him. *Does he want me to say the simple one? Which one does he want me to pick?*

He said, "The diamonds, boy, look at the diamonds."

I looked, and the one I chose and the one I'll be using tonight has diamonds on it to show the reverence for the Eucharist, to show the reverence for the wine that will become the blood of Christ, the wine that will become something that goes into ourselves and helps us to live our lives in the way God wants us to live them.

One time we were driving, and I was the one driving his car. He said to me, "Go around the block another time."

And I asked, "Why do you want me to go around the block another time?"

He answered, "Because you missed a few potholes the first time."

I laughed. Some people remind us that we are human. There are people in our lives who are important.

Monsignor said to me one day, "Don't be proud of doing something that you're supposed to do." The sentence was kind of tough. I do not remember what we were talking about.

I was probably saying, "I was listening to God, and I was praying so I would make the right decisions."

And he said to me, "Don't be proud of doing something you're supposed to do."

How many times are we proud of doing something we should be doing anyway?

The last line of the gospel said, "we are unprofitable servants; we have done what we were obliged to do". This is Respect Life Sunday. Each one of us is called to respect life in all its forms and in whatever situation we find ourselves. Now there are some lives we want to respect more than other lives, even if God wants us to respect all equally. Some people are easier to respect than other people. There are some situations where we find ourselves able to show the face of Christ. Sometimes I wonder if we think we are not obliged to show respect to life in all situations. That is something we can choose whether we want to do it or not.

I remember what Monsignor Shaw said, "Don't be proud of doing the things you were supposed to do."

Anyway, this gospel is a difficult one. Jesus asks, "Who among you would ask your servant ... 'Come here immediately and take your place at table'?" Jesus isn't saying we should be mean to people, we shouldn't be good to people, or we should treat people like servants. What Jesus is telling us is, if you have a job to do and you do that job, then there's nothing great in that. You're doing the job you are supposed to do, and that's good. Maybe we can look at it differently.

What parent would say to their kids, "You know, tonight you're in charge. You can do whatever you want tonight, and you can tell us what to do because we're going to switch roles completely"?

The parents here are saying, "Oh no, I'm not going to do that!" Maybe some of our younger people here would like that tonight. "You know, tonight we're going to be in charge, and you're not going to be in charge." **Ultimately, God is always in charge.** In the end, we must try to figure out, "What does God want us to do? How does God want us to live?" And then we simply ask for the grace to do so.

In the beginning of the gospel, the apostles say to Jesus, "Increase our faith." Jesus basically says that we do not need to increase our faith because we already have enough faith. **Jesus says, "If you have faith the size of a mustard seed, you would say to this mulberry tree, 'be uprooted and planted in the sea,' and it would obey you."** Do you know how small a mustard seed is?! Sometimes we think we need more faith, but if we just look inside of ourselves, He is there. He lives inside each one of us. **He gives each one of us the grace and the strength we need.**

The second reading said, "Beloved: I remind you to stir into flame the gift of God that you have through the imposition of my hands." Stir into flame! In other words, there is something we must do. We can't just sit back and say, "Okay, Lord, you do whatever you need to do. I'm just going to sit here." There is something we need to do. We do not have to worry about what that something is because God will show us if we pay attention. The reading goes on to say, "For God did not give us a spirit of cowardice, but rather, one of power and love and self-control." When the Spirit is dwelling within us and we recognize that Spirit, we might still be afraid, but we're able to push through that fear because we know God's working with us and we are able to use His power. We can use His love. We can use His self-control. If there is one thing we could pray for every day and it would help us across the board, it is probably self-control. Self-control helps us stop and think about what we say and do when certain things happen. If we just had self-control, we would be able to make better choices, to do the things God wants us to do. How we have self-control is by asking God each day, "God, give me self-control today." Do not be ashamed of your testimony to Our Lord. Most of us are not ashamed. For the most part, most of us are not going to turn our backs on the Lord. But maybe there are times when, in just a little way, we do not necessarily want to show Christ to others.

The other night we had our "Snacking with Scripture" meeting, and we talked about meals and when you go into a restaurant and see people praying before they eat their meal. I wonder how often we do that. It is a simple way to be a testimony to others, but many times, we just do not think about it. What a witness it can be to be sitting in the middle of a restaurant, making the sign of the cross, saying grace, and then making the sign of the cross. It is not that we are necessarily ashamed of our faith. We just ask God for the grace to be able to share that with others, **"bear your share of hardships for the Gospel with the strength that comes from God."** The way we respect life is to deal with whatever hardships come, knowing we are not walking alone and knowing God is there.

The first reading said, "How long, O Lord? I cry for help but You do not listen!" I imagine all of us can think of at least a time when we've cried out to God saying, "How long, Lord? You are not paying attention. You're not listening." In the middle of the reading, God assures us He is with us even though you may not think He is listening. He is here, and He is always going to be here. He reminds us we might not think He is here, but He is! It is okay for us to think God's not listening. **That is okay. But when we have those thoughts, that is when we tell God, "God, I'm going to trust You."**

The psalm says, "If today you hear His Voice, harden not your hearts." To hear His voice, we need to listen. Maybe the best way we can do what we are obliged to do is just by listening and paying attention. As Monsignor Shaw said to me, "Don't be proud of doing the things you're supposed to do anyway," and in no way was he saying not to be happy about making good choices. Simply recognize certain things we are naturally supposed to do. **In our lives, if we truly are followers of God, if we genuinely want one day to spend all of eternity with Him, then we are going to do what God wants us to do. He will help us to figure out how we are supposed to respect life and one another. He will give us that spirit of strength so we will not be afraid.** Even amid fear, we will be able to push through it because we know God is there. The Lord dwells within each one of us. He wants to be a part of everything we do. **All we need to do is allow Him.**

READINGS FOR OCTOBER 13, 2019

First Reading
2 Kings 5:14–17

Naaman went down and plunged into the Jordan seven times
at the word of Elisha, the man of God.
His flesh became again like the flesh of a little child,
and he was clean of his leprosy.
Naaman returned with his whole retinue to the man of God.
On his arrival he stood before Elisha and said,
"Now I know that there is no God in all the earth,
except in Israel.
Please accept a gift from your servant."
Elisha replied, "As the LORD lives whom I serve, I will not take it";
and despite Naaman's urging, he still refused.
Naaman said: "If you will not accept,
please let me, your servant, have two mule-loads of earth,
for I will no longer offer holocaust or sacrifice
to any other god except to the LORD."

Responsorial Psalm
Psalm 98: 1–4

R. The Lord has revealed to the nations his saving power.

Sing to the LORD a new song,
for he has done wondrous deeds;
his right hand has won victory for him,
his holy arm. **R.**

The LORD has made his salvation known:
in the sight of the nations he has revealed his justice.
He has remembered his kindness and his faithfulness
toward the house of Israel. **R.**

All the ends of the earth have seen
the salvation by our God.
Sing joyfully to the LORD, all you lands:
break into song; sing praise. **R.**

Second Reading
2 Timothy 2:8–13

Beloved:
Remember Jesus Christ, raised from the dead, a descendant of David:
such is my gospel, for which I am suffering,
even to the point of chains, like a criminal.
But the word of God is not chained.
Therefore, I bear with everything for the sake of those who are chosen,
so that they too may obtain the salvation that is in Christ Jesus,
together with eternal glory.
This saying is trustworthy:
If we have died with him
we shall also live with him;
if we persevere
we shall also reign with him.
But if we deny him
he will deny us.
If we are unfaithful
he remains faithful,
for he cannot deny himself.

Gospel
Luke 17:11–19

As Jesus continued his journey to Jerusalem,
he traveled through Samaria and Galilee.
As he was entering a village, ten lepers met him.
They stood at a distance from him and raised their voices, saying,
"Jesus, Master! Have pity on us!"
And when he saw them, he said,
"Go show yourselves to the priests."
As they were going they were cleansed.
And one of them, realizing he had been healed,
returned, glorifying God in a loud voice;
and he fell at the feet of Jesus and thanked him.
He was a Samaritan.
Jesus said in reply,

"Ten were cleansed, were they not?
Where are the other nine?
Has none but this foreigner returned to give thanks to God?"
Then he said to him, "Stand up and go;
your faith has saved you."

"Faith Is Trusting His Direction without Knowing Our Destination"

HOMILY GIVEN ON OCTOBER 13, 2019

About a week ago, I was playing golf, and as I was standing on the first tee ready to hit my first shot, I swung my driver, and my driver head broke off the golf club! It flew this way, and my golf ball flew in another direction. I was left standing there holding the shaft mumbling, "What just happened?" I did not know whether I should follow the direction of the club head or the direction of the golf ball itself.

I wonder how many times in life we feel that same way! We feel pulled, and we don't know in which direction we are supposed to go. We just find ourselves floundering, trying to figure out what we are supposed to do. It is a good thing that GPS was invented because, if you are a guy like me who isn't going to ask for directions, a GPS will just plug in the address and point you exactly where you are supposed to go and let you know how long it will take with the amount of traffic present on that route.

Sometimes in life, we do not know which direction we are supposed to go, but the one who gives us direction is Jesus Christ Himself. When we are tempted to go this way but Jesus wants us to go another way, He will let us know. Sometimes we think, *Well no, He's not there. I don't hear Him. I don't know what I'm supposed to do.* We just have to pause and include

Him, especially in those times when we are not exactly sure which way we should go.

I have a pillow in my house, and on the pillow is written, "Faith is trusting His direction without knowing our destination." "Faith is trusting His direction without knowing our destination." We hear all the time that we are supposed to trust in God. It is one thing to trust in God if we know exactly what is going to happen, if we know exactly what direction we are called to take, and if we know what is going to be at the other end. However, it is a bit more difficult to trust in God's direction when we do not know what or where the destination is.

One of the many ways we as Catholics are blessed is by receiving the Eucharist. Through this sacrament, we are able to feel God's presence in such a way that we can trust that He is leading us in the direction that is best for us. **When we consume His body and His blood, we truly allow Him to become part of us and allow Him to be a part of everything we are!** However, after Mass, we can merely just continue with our day or ask Him to truly give direction to our lives.

In the gospel, we hear the story of the ten lepers who are cured, but only one comes back and is grateful. I wonder where we could be a little more grateful in our lives. Sometimes, when we are in the moment, it's hard to be grateful, but when we look back and, if we are honest, we can see God's presence in our lives and know that He was there.

Leprosy is a terrible disease. Most of us probably have never been in the presence of someone who has leprosy. But I wonder what it is that we need to be healed from. I wonder in a sense what our leprosy is. Maybe it is simply just not trusting enough in God. Perhaps it is simply not trusting that He is giving direction to our lives or we are not trusting the direction He is giving us.

The second reading said if we have died with Him and if we persevere, if we remain faithful, then He will remain faithful to us. But even if we do not remain faithful, He is still going to be faithful to us! I wonder what God might be asking us to do today. What is going on in our hearts? What is going on in our lives that we need to die to so we can allow the Lord to take its place? How is the Lord calling us to persevere and we are not sure we are able to do it? Where is the Lord asking us to trust that He is with us and that He will take care of us no matter what happens? Where is God calling us to be faithful? Are we finding it difficult to have faith? There is no way God can promise everything is going to turn out exactly the way we want it to, but He does promise to be present and give direction to our lives. **"With God all things are possible."**

In the beginning of the second reading, St. Paul talks about suffering. He was able to see that there was value in his suffering, and in the midst of his suffering, he grew closer to the Lord. All of us suffer in one way or another. Sometimes our sufferings are right out there for everybody to see, and other times they are just inside us, they are not visible, and others do not know. We can choose to allow the Lord to give us direction in the midst of our suffering, in the midst of our difficulties.

The title of our opening song today is "Sing a New Song unto The Lord." What "new song" might the Lord be asking us to sing today? Maybe that new song is "Lord, I'm going to follow Your direction in my life. I'm not just going to try to be my own GPS and my own leader. I'm going to trust in Your direction, even if I don't know the destination." Perhaps that is the "new song!"

In the first reading, we heard of Naaman who does as Elisha, the man of God, tells him, and we're told he plunged himself into the water. This was a highly active thing. So many times we just want to sit back and let God do everything. But as in this incident, God wants Naaman to put a little action into it himself. Then Naaman is healed. We are told, "his flesh became again like the flesh of a little child." If we could go back in time and be little children again, I wonder what we would change. The reality is, no matter what we come up with, we are who we were then, we are who we are now, and we can only change things going forward. Our flesh can be made anew going forward only if we allow the Lord to give direction to our lives.

So I wasn't sure what I was going to do in my golf game without my driver, but I survived. I use the GPS for directions, but the Lord Jesus wants to be our GPS: He wants to be the One who guides us through our life. **Faith is trusting His direction without knowing our destination, and we trust in the Lord's direction even when we're not sure where He is leading us.**

READINGS FOR OCTOBER 20, 2019

First Reading
Exodus 17:8–13

In those days, Amalek came and waged war against Israel.
Moses, therefore, said to Joshua,
"Pick out certain men,
and tomorrow go out and engage Amalek in battle.
I will be standing on top of the hill
with the staff of God in my hand."
So Joshua did as Moses told him:
he engaged Amalek in battle
after Moses had climbed to the top of the hill with Aaron and Hur.
As long as Moses kept his hands raised up,
Israel had the better of the fight,
but when he let his hands rest,
Amalek had the better of the fight.
Moses' hands, however, grew tired;
so they put a rock in place for him to sit on.
Meanwhile Aaron and Hur supported his hands,
one on one side and one on the other,
so that his hands remained steady till sunset.
And Joshua mowed down Amalek and his people
with the edge of the sword.

Responsorial Psalm
Psalm 121:1–8

R. Our help is from the Lord, who made heaven and earth.
I lift up my eyes toward the mountains;
whence shall help come to me?
My help is from the LORD,
who made heaven and earth. **R.**

May he not suffer your foot to slip;
may he slumber not who guards you:
indeed he neither slumbers nor sleeps,
the guardian of Israel. **R.**

The LORD is your guardian; the LORD is your shade;
he is beside you at your right hand.
The sun shall not harm you by day,
nor the moon by night. **R.**

The LORD will guard you from all evil;
he will guard your life.
The LORD will guard your coming and your going,
both now and forever. **R.**

Second Reading
2 Timothy 3:14–4:2
Beloved:
Remain faithful to what you have learned and believed,
because you know from whom you learned it,
and that from infancy you have known the sacred Scriptures,
which are capable of giving you wisdom for salvation
through faith in Christ Jesus.
All Scripture is inspired by God
and is useful for teaching, for refutation, for correction,
and for training in righteousness,
so that one who belongs to God may be competent,
equipped for every good work.
I charge you in the presence of God and of Christ Jesus,
who will judge the living and the dead,
and by his appearing and his kingly power:
proclaim the word;
be persistent whether it is convenient or inconvenient;
convince, reprimand, encourage through all patience and teaching.

Gospel
Luke 18:1–8
Jesus told his disciples a parable
about the necessity for them to pray always without becoming weary.
He said, "There was a judge in a certain town
who neither feared God nor respected any human being.

And a widow in that town used to come to him and say,
'Render a just decision for me against my adversary.'
For a long time the judge was unwilling, but eventually he thought,
'While it is true that I neither fear God nor respect any human being,
because this widow keeps bothering me
I shall deliver a just decision for her
lest she finally come and strike me.'"
The Lord said, "Pay attention to what the dishonest judge says.
Will not God then secure the rights of his chosen ones
who call out to him day and night?
Will he be slow to answer them?
I tell you, he will see to it that justice is done for them speedily.
But when the Son of Man comes, will he find faith on earth?"

Sacred Scripture:
Let God Talk to Your Heart

HOMILY GIVEN ON OCTOBER 20, 2019

So I have a couple of Bibles sitting here. Many of us had a Bible growing up. My family's sat on a coffee table, and every day we walked past it. But this isn't what the Bible looked like when I was growing up. The cover of the Bible has been changed. Somebody offered to go and get the cover of the Bible fixed for me, and unfortunately it came back with the original cover completely gone, and this second cover replaced it on our family Bible.

The other day I went to see if I could get the cover on this Bible transferred to the cover on the original family Bible so it would then be the Bible I remembered growing up with as a kid. Sadly, I was told the original cover could not be saved because it could not be taken off and reused. The salesperson told me that many Bibles looking exactly like mine were widely sold in the 1950s. As a matter of fact, some of you may have a Bible that looks like the one I had. Inside, there are all kinds of interesting pictures, but what is most interesting is, in the one that is my family Bible, there is a section with all the family history including, but not limited to, anniversaries and births of many of our relatives before my parents going back many years. It's just a great Bible to have around!

I wonder how many of us had a family Bible. How many of us had a Bible that was sitting somewhere in the house that you passed each day and is now a great memory. It is one of my greatest memories that I have of growing up, seeing that Bible daily. I must admit, though, I am not sure I ever remember us opening that Bible, but I knew that it was sitting there, and it made a great impact on me. So the first thing I invite all to do is to make sure there is a Bible visible in your home. Make it visible to your family. Go to Google. I'm sure you can purchase one. If possible, purchase one that has a place where you can put all the family history and display it in your home.

I also wonder if families who have Bibles open them. Do we have a Bible that we open? Do we have a Bible that we read? There was a time when the church would tell us to be careful reading the Scriptures because the church did not want us to misinterpret the Scriptures. However, the church today would say, "**Read the Scriptures. Let God talk to your heart.** Let God go deep within you and let the Scriptures be a gateway to grow closer to the Lord. Just be aware that there might be a meaning in those Scriptures that is a little different than what you are hearing. Still, that does not mean God's not speaking to you."

In the second reading today, we heard, "All Scripture is inspired by God and is useful for teaching, for refutation, for correction, and for training in righteousness." Further, "from infancy you have known the **Sacred Scriptures, which are capable of giving you wisdom for salvation through faith in Christ Jesus**."

Maybe we don't open the Bible because we don't necessarily want the Bible to speak to us. Maybe we don't open the Scriptures because we are afraid we might read something and see something that might make us have to do things a little bit differently. So if I come to church, listen to the sermon, and listen to the readings being read at Mass, then that's good enough. I don't really need to go any deeper. Imagine, possibly sometime this week, we decided to read a page a day, ten verses a day, or two chapters of Sacred Scripture! Maybe we start with one of the gospels. We're reading Luke right now. Just take time to read and slowly work your way through the Scriptures and we may be surprised.

We may be surprised just how God speaks to us, just how God is trying to communicate with us, "proclaim the Word, be persistent whether it is convenient or inconvenient." Sometimes following the Lord is very convenient. It's extremely easy. "He doesn't ask much of us. Yeah, I can do that. Yeah, this is what the Lord wants me to do. I feel pretty confident with that." However, sometimes following the Lord can be very inconvenient. "Everyone else is doing it. Let's do it." But you know you should say, "No!" Sometimes what the Lord asks of us is a little more difficult than we are willing to handle.

In the gospel, the dishonest judge finally agrees to what the widow wants because she is just driving him to distraction, he doesn't want to be bothered anymore, and most likely, he would just give in eventually anyway. Imagine how much greater God will be with us! Imagine how much more He wants us to be persistent with Him! God is not up there just wanting us to be quiet! No, instead He wants us to keep talking to him, talking and praying to him unceasingly. **Pray, always pray without becoming weary.** Oftentimes we just get weary. We get tired and may think, *I ask God for the same thing repeatedly, and nothing seems to happen.* We just get tired, you know, asking God for the same thing over and over again and nothing seems to happen. How much do we see that in the Scriptures, in the Old and New Testaments, people praying for things and the prayers seem not to be answered?

Perhaps tonight God wants us to stay on course, to keep being persistent and not give up because it might seem like, right now, He is not answering our prayer. But He is here, He is present, and He hears our cries. It is possible we think we are listening, but in reality, we do not understand that God knows everything about our lives. Sometimes we can get so focused on thinking this is the only place we are ever going to be, but one day we can be with Him in heaven. **Things down here can sometimes make us weary. But God has much greater plans.**

We are reminded in the psalm, "Our help is from the Lord, who made heaven and earth." Could it be that our God, who made heaven and earth, may just be able to take care of us? If He could make heaven and earth, then He can create everything that exists. Maybe He **is** paying attention, and maybe I can keep praying. **Maybe I can take a chance and open the Bible and read Scripture and allow the Lord to touch my heart.**

In the first reading, we hear about Moses. While he had his arms up with the staff of God in his hands and with God's grace working through him, he was able to do amazing things and help the soldiers. However, whenever his arms went down, things became much more difficult.

Perhaps the Bible is our "Staff of God." Maybe that is what helps us to continue being able to trust God, to stay close to Him, and to keep being persistent. Maybe, when we get weary, it is the Lord Jesus Christ in Sacred Scriptures who wants to hold up our arms. **When we feel weak, He is there to support our arms and keep our bodies erect. He is there to take care of us!**

My family Bible is still the same. Even though it has a different cover on it, it still has the same history and the same meaning. Maybe tonight we can ask ourselves, "Do I have a place where I can keep a Bible to remind me that the source of everything we are is the Lord Jesus Christ?" He is the source of everything we are. Maybe tonight there will be a run on Bibles. Who knows? Maybe we can take a chance and open the Bible? Start with the New Testament? Perhaps with Luke? If we just read a little each day, we might be amazed at the power that God can give us. **Do not become weary. Stay persistent. May we trust in God's presence, even when we wonder where He is, because He is here, He is present, and He wants to be our strength.**

READINGS FOR OCTOBER 27, 2019

First Reading
Sirach 35:12–14, 16–18
The LORD is a God of justice,
who knows no favorites.
Though not unduly partial toward the weak,
yet he hears the cry of the oppressed.
The Lord is not deaf to the wail of the orphan,
nor to the widow when she pours out her complaint.
The one who serves God willingly is heard;
his petition reaches the heavens.
The prayer of the lowly pierces the clouds;
it does not rest till it reaches its goal,
nor will it withdraw till the Most High responds,
judges justly and affirms the right,
and the Lord will not delay.

Responsorial Psalm
Psalm 34:2–3, 17–19, 23
R. The Lord hears the cry of the poor.
I will bless the LORD at all times;
his praise shall be ever in my mouth.
Let my soul glory in the LORD;
the lowly will hear me and be glad. **R.**

The LORD confronts the evildoers,
to destroy remembrance of them from the earth.
When the just cry out, the LORD hears them,
and from all their distress he rescues them. **R.**

The LORD is close to the brokenhearted;
and those who are crushed in spirit he saves.
The LORD redeems the lives of his servants;
no one incurs guilt who takes refuge in him. **R.**

Second Reading
2 Timothy 4:6–8, 16–18
Beloved:
I am already being poured out like a libation,
and the time of my departure is at hand.
I have competed well; I have finished the race;
I have kept the faith.
From now on the crown of righteousness awaits me,
which the Lord, the just judge,
will award to me on that day, and not only to me,
but to all who have longed for his appearance.
At my first defense no one appeared on my behalf,
but everyone deserted me.
May it not be held against them!
But the Lord stood by me and gave me strength,
so that through me the proclamation might be completed
and all the Gentiles might hear it.
And I was rescued from the lion's mouth.
The Lord will rescue me from every evil threat
and will bring me safe to his heavenly kingdom.
To him be glory forever and ever. Amen.

Gospel
Luke 18:9–14
Jesus addressed this parable
to those who were convinced of their own righteousness
and despised everyone else.
"Two people went up to the temple area to pray;
one was a Pharisee and the other was a tax collector.
The Pharisee took up his position and spoke this prayer to himself,
'O God, I thank you that I am not like the rest of humanity—
greedy, dishonest, adulterous—or even like this tax collector.
I fast twice a week, and I pay tithes on my whole income.'
But the tax collector stood off at a distance
and would not even raise his eyes to heaven
but beat his breast and prayed,

'O God, be merciful to me a sinner.'
I tell you, the latter went home justified, not the former;
for whoever exalts himself will be humbled,
and the one who humbles himself will be exalted."

The Strength to Believe

HOMILY GIVEN ON OCTOBER 27, 2019

I PUT TOGETHER A LIST OF THINGS FROM DIFFERENT SOURCES THAT ARE hard to believe.

- Lobsters don't grow old and never die. In fact, as far as scientists can tell, they only die of external causes. I am not sure if I would never want to grow old and never die. Maybe there is a part of us that says, "No, that would be wonderful!" Who would have thought that lobsters never grow old? That is hard to believe!
- Honey does not spoil. You could feasibly eat five thousand-year-old honey! I do not know which of us would want to volunteer to do that, but we could eat honey that is five thousand years old!
- A full head of human hair is strong enough to support twelve tons. I will never find that out since I am bald, but maybe one of you will find that out. Can you imagine trying to support twelve tons with human hair?
- If you could fold a piece of paper in half forty-two times, it would reach the moon. Now that doesn't make any sense at all! Obviously I do not even think you can try that.
- Snails have fourteen thousand teeth. I did not know they had one tooth, let alone fourteen thousand!
- The human nose can remember fifty thousand different scents. Fifty thousand scents are hard to believe! And we can remember

every time somebody did anything to us, anytime somebody hurt us!
- Bullfrogs do not sleep. This one I am not so sure about.
- The TV was invented only two years after the invention of sliced bread. That has got to be impossible!
- The record for solving the Rubik's Cube is 4.22 seconds.
- The most popular item sold at Walmart is bananas. They sell more bananas than any other item they stock.
- This last item is a little scary for Ohio residents. If you live in Ohio, the state distributes different colored license plates for those convicted of DUI. Then I am not sure if I want, or do not want, to live in Ohio!

Many different things are hard to believe. When it comes to church, when it comes to our Catholic faith, perhaps one of the things that is most difficult to believe is that ordinary bread and wine becomes the body and blood of Jesus. How many times have we heard that? How many times in a homily do we hear that ordinary bread and wine become the body and blood of Jesus during Mass? If we really believe that, if we really have internalized that, every time we come up and receive Our Lord in the Eucharist, it would change us. We would live our lives differently. We would deal with situations differently. Maybe one of the things on that list is easier to believe than the body and blood of Jesus, but what is good for us to remember is the reason we gather, the reason we are here as brothers and sisters in Christ, to gather around this table and receive the Lord.

The first reading today also speaks about something that is hard to believe, that the Lord "knows no favorites." Maybe there are times that we think, *No, I think God does have favorites, and I'm not one of them.* The reading goes on to say, **"Though not unduly partial toward the weak, yet He hears the cry of the oppressed." He is not deaf. He does hear.** Maybe there are times it's hard for us to believe God wants to be a part of each one of our lives. He truly wants to be involved in **each** of our lives, not just the life of someone sitting next to us.

How can God possibly be involved in every one of our lives? If we all stopped right now and prayed, how could He possibly pay attention to all of us? Maybe that is one of the most difficult things to believe, that God really wants to be involved and He **can** be involved. **After receiving Our Lord in the Eucharist, we have the strength to then believe He wants to be a part of our lives and He wants to dwell within us, and even if we do not understand it, God truly is a part of everything that we are!**

"The one who serves God is willingly heard" and "the prayer of the lowly pierces the clouds," what a wonderful image that is! The prayer from the very depths of our souls goes right through the clouds and up to God. Somehow He truly does hear us. Perhaps what we heard in the psalm today about hope is speaking to us, "The Lord hears the cry of the poor," "I will bless the Lord at all times, His Praise shall be ever in my mouth," "When the just cry out, the Lord hears them," and "The Lord is close to the brokenhearted." **We have hope.**

There are times in our lives when the hardest thing for us to believe is that we can have hope, especially during periods of trials and difficulties. In the second reading, St. Paul says, "I am already being poured out like a libation ... I have competed well; I have finished the race; I have kept the faith." What is interesting is that St. Paul said, "I have finished the race." He did not say he won the race. Each day, we wake up, get out of bed, and go through the day. We can choose whether we are going to compete during the day, whether we are going to keep trusting that God is there, or whether we are going to give up. Nowhere in the Bible does God say we have to win the race. He just tells us to finish the race. The way we finish the race is by believing. Even when it is most difficult to believe, He truly is with us. Paul goes on to say, "But the Lord stood by me and gave me strength." Do we believe that? Do we believe right now that the Lord is standing by us and giving us strength, or do we find that hard to believe?

In the gospel, "Jesus addressed this parable to those who were convinced of their own righteousness and despised everyone else." For sure, none of us fall into that category (Fr. Dan winks), but maybe there are times we are convinced of our own righteousness. Maybe in hard times we look down on other people. Possibly we pray the prayer of the Pharisee who said, "Oh God, I thank You. I'm not like everybody else." Perhaps we stop and think, *I would never say that prayer.* But there are times we do say, "God, I am glad I'm not like everybody else." The tax collector said, "O God be merciful to me, a sinner." What is this, an act of humility!? The last line of the gospel says, "For whoever exalts himself will be humbled, and the one who humbles himself will be exalted." **If we genuinely believe that God is present, then we are willing to humble ourselves before Him and allow Him to be food for our journey.**

The list of things that are hard for us to believe is long, but hopefully for us, we will find it easier to believe as we discover the truth of bread and wine becoming the body and blood of Jesus. Jesus truly does care about us and wants to be a part of everything we are. **He does hear our cries. May we be willing to humble ourselves before the Lord and allow Him to be "food for our journey."**

READINGS FOR NOVEMBER 3, 2019

First Reading
Wisdom 11:22–12:2
Before the LORD the whole universe is as a grain from a balance
or a drop of morning dew come down upon the earth.
But you have mercy on all, because you can do all things;
and you overlook people's sins that they may repent.
For you love all things that are
and loathe nothing that you have made;
for what you hated, you would not have fashioned.
And how could a thing remain, unless you willed it;
or be preserved, had it not been called forth by you?
But you spare all things, because they are yours,
O LORD and lover of souls,
for your imperishable spirit is in all things!
Therefore you rebuke offenders little by little,
warn them and remind them of the sins they are committing,
that they may abandon their wickedness and believe in you, O LORD!

Responsorial Psalm
Psalm 145:1–2, 8–11, 13–14
R. I will praise your name forever, my king and my God.
I will extol you, O my God and King,
and I will bless your name forever and ever.
Every day will I bless you,
and I will praise your name forever and ever. **R.**

The LORD is gracious and merciful,
slow to anger and of great kindness.
The LORD is good to all
and compassionate toward all his works. **R.**

Let all your works give you thanks, O LORD,
and let your faithful ones bless you.
Let them discourse of the glory of your kingdom
and speak of your might. **R.**

The LORD is faithful in all his words
and holy in all his works.
The LORD lifts up all who are falling
and raises up all who are bowed down. **R.**

Second Reading
2 Thessalonians 1:11–2:2
Brothers and sisters:
We always pray for you,
that our God may make you worthy of his calling
and powerfully bring to fulfillment every good purpose
and every effort of faith,
that the name of our Lord Jesus may be glorified in you,
and you in him,
in accord with the grace of our God and Lord Jesus Christ.
We ask you, brothers and sisters,
with regard to the coming of our Lord Jesus Christ
and our assembling with him,
not to be shaken out of your minds suddenly, or to be alarmed
either by a "spirit," or by an oral statement,
or by a letter allegedly from us
to the effect that the day of the Lord is at hand.

Gospel
Luke 19:1–10
At that time, Jesus came to Jericho and
intended to pass through the town.
Now a man there named Zacchaeus,
who was a chief tax collector and also a wealthy man,
was seeking to see who Jesus was;
but he could not see him because of the crowd,
for he was short in stature.
So he ran ahead and climbed a sycamore tree in order to see Jesus,
who was about to pass that way.
When he reached the place, Jesus looked up and said,
"Zacchaeus, come down quickly,

for today I must stay at your house."
And he came down quickly and received him with joy.
When they all saw this, they began to grumble, saying,
"He has gone to stay at the house of a sinner."
But Zacchaeus stood there and said to the Lord,
"Behold, half of my possessions, Lord, I shall give to the poor,
and if I have extorted anything from anyone
I shall repay it four times over."
And Jesus said to him,
"Today salvation has come to this house
because this man too is a descendant of Abraham.
For the Son of Man has come to seek
and to save what was lost."

Called by Name

HOMILY GIVEN ON NOVEMBER 3, 2019

Yesterday morning, I said Mass at the Padre Pio National Center in Bartow, Pennsylvania. If you do not know where Bartow, Pennsylvania, is, go up to Reading and then just drive around a little bit, and you eventually get to Bartow. Today is the thirty-first Sunday in Ordinary Time, but yesterday was All Souls Day, a day when we remember all those people who have died. We pray for them that they are with God in His heavenly homeland, and we ask them to pray for us also. Padre Pio was known to have a special relationship with the holy souls, and it is said that people from purgatory came and visited with Padre Pio who spoke with them. If you want to check that out, go to Google, and you will see that the stories abound. Today, I just want to share a few things about St. Padre Pio who offered his pains, prayers, and sufferings for the release of those in a state of purification, and those souls never cease to thank him for this.

Sometimes we look at purgatory and think, *The church just made that up*. The church did not just make it up. The church explains that we believe in heaven and hell, but when someone dies who has not quite atoned for their sins, a stay in purgatory is needed. Time spent in purgatory is time spent purging oneself of those things that might have kept one from being able to see God completely. So Padre Pio believed that the pains and sufferings he endured could be offered for people who had died, and we too can do the same thing. Padre Pio allowed the Lord Jesus Christ to enter deep within his suffering and indeed almost penetrated it. We too can invite God deep within our suffering, deep within our pain. So many times, we say to God, "Get rid of this. I don't want this anymore." That is true, and we all have probably said that. But perhaps we can invite God into the pain and suffering and ask Him to dwell deep within whatever is troubling us, whatever trials we have. Then in the midst of those trials, perhaps we can feel His strength even deeper. "Do as I have done," Padre Pio says. "Pray always for the souls of the dearly departed." We can pray for those who have died, and it does make a difference. We believe, if it does not make a difference in their eternal life because they are already with God completely, it makes a difference in somebody else's life who needs those prayers. Padre Pio said of heaven, "Heaven is total joy, continuous joy. We will be constantly thanking God. It is useless to try to figure out exactly what heaven is like because we cannot understand it. But, when the veil of this life is taken off, we will understand things in a different way. You will be surprised to find souls in paradise you never expected to be there."

Makes you think, doesn't it? I love that statement because I wonder how many people I will be surprised to see there! It also assumes, "We are going there, but they are going somewhere else?!" That is why it is good for us to stay connected. When we pray for people who have gone before us, it just keeps us all connected. Padre Pio said, "I believe that not a great number of souls, not a great number, go to hell. God loves us so much. He formed us in His image. God loves us beyond understanding and it is my belief that, when we have passed from the consciousness of this world, when we appear to be dead, God, before He judges us, will give us a chance to see and understand what sin really is, and, if we understand it properly, how could we fail to repent?"

For me, that brings great hope that, no matter where we are in this life, God is there with His arms reaching out to us in His infinite love, mercy, and forgiveness. That is why how we live in this world is so important! How we live here affects how we live in the next.

Padre Pio was made a saint in 2002. Someone once asked St. Pio, "How can purgatory be avoided?" and he said, "By accepting everything from God's hands and offering everything up to Him with love and thanksgiving, this will enable us to pass from our deathbed to Paradise." Offering everything up to God? Maybe that is just quite simply saying,

"God, you know what is going on, what is happening in my life. I give it all to You. I trust You are walking with me. Give me Your grace." It sounds nice and easy to say it, but not necessarily easy to do!

In the first reading, we heard, "Before the Lord, the whole universe is as a grain from a balance or a drop of morning dew." This means we are as small as a grain of sand or a drop of water placed on a scale that makes no difference in weight whatsoever. That is how big the universe is when it comes to God, but He cares about every one of us, and He loves each one of us. "But You spare all things because they are Yours, O Lord, Lover of Souls." **He wants to overlook what we have done. He wants to forgive us.** Sometimes we are the ones that beat ourselves up. We are the ones that hold onto things or we remind others of the sins they are committing so they may abandon their wickedness and believe in You but fail to look at ourselves. Maybe that is a prayer we need to make, not just for ourselves but for our world. **A revelation to our world that believing in the Lord, a belief in something greater, is important.**

The psalm said, "I will praise Your Name forever and ever." That is a long time! It is not just forever. It is forever and ever. It is a long time! That is how much God loves us, and He wants to be with us forever and ever. At the end of the psalm, it said, "The Lord lifts up all who are falling." It does not say the Lord lifts all who fell, but "the Lord lifts up all who are falling." We are in the process of falling, and the Lord wants to catch us. Maybe we find ourselves in the position tonight where we are falling. We just do not know what is going on, and that image of the Lord catching us reminds us that this is what He wants to do "and raises up all who are bowed down." **So when we go before the Lord humbly and say, "Lord, it is in Your Hands," then He can raise us up.**

The second reading said, "Brothers and Sisters, We always pray for you." Praying for one another does make a difference. Not sure about you, but when someone says, "I am praying for you," it makes a difference because somebody else cares. It does make a difference. We also pray for those who have died. That means somebody else cares and the deceased are not forgotten. Yesterday was All Souls Day, which is all about not being forgotten.

In the gospel, the Lord says to Zacchaeus, "come down (from tree) quickly." Jesus does not want him to be shaken out of his faith but wants to

Sunday Snippets from Fr. Dan

dwell in Zacchaeus. Jesus wants to be part of him. Sometimes the things of this world shake us. Sometimes the things that happened in our life shake us. But do not be shaken suddenly because, **as Jesus called Zacchaeus by name, so He also calls each one of us by name.** We get the sense that Jesus had never met Zacchaeus before, but He knew him, and He knows each one of us. We are told the people grumbled, "He has gone to stay at the house of a sinner." I wonder how many times we grumble, "Look at that person. Look at this person." Maybe, even sometimes when we look in the mirror, we grumble, "Oh, look at," but maybe we don't have to feel that way! The Lord wants to be my strength and to guide me when in despair. He wants to hold me in the palm of His hand. If we are honest, most of us, if not all of us, can think of some time when God picked us up when we were falling. He was right there, ready to pick us up. Zacchaeus stood and said, "Half of my possessions, Lord, I shall give to the poor and if I have extorted anything from anyone I shall repay it four times over." In response to this, Jesus says, "Salvation has come to this house." This is our house (Fr. Dan points to himself), and this is God's house. **He wants to bring salvation to this house. He wants to be a part of all that we are. It is up to us.**

St. Padre Pio had a real connection with the soul, with holy souls, and, whether we want to believe it or not, with the souls in purgatory. We are told that he visited them and he prayed for them and that they pray for us. We are connected to all those who have gone before us. Today, we pray for the grace and the strength to believe and to trust in the Lord, to trust that He does love us, to trust that He loves every one of us and wants to share His gift of eternal life. May we pray for one another! **Pray for one another. Pray for those who have died, and do not be afraid to ask those who have died to pray for us.**

READINGS FOR NOVEMBER 10, 2019

First Reading
2 Maccabees 7:1–2, 9–14

It happened that seven brothers with their mother were arrested
and tortured with whips and scourges by the king,
to force them to eat pork in violation of God's law.
One of the brothers, speaking for the others, said:
"What do you expect to achieve by questioning us?
We are ready to die rather than transgress the laws of our ancestors."
At the point of death he said:
"You accursed fiend, you are depriving us of this present life,
but the King of the world will raise us up to live again forever.
It is for his laws that we are dying."
After him the third suffered their cruel sport.
He put out his tongue at once when told to do so,
and bravely held out his hands, as he spoke these noble words:
"It was from Heaven that I received these;
for the sake of his laws I disdain them;
from him I hope to receive them again."
Even the king and his attendants marveled at the young man's courage,
because he regarded his sufferings as nothing.
After he had died,
they tortured and maltreated the fourth brother in the same way.
When he was near death, he said,
"It is my choice to die at the hands of men
with the hope God gives of being raised up by him;
but for you, there will be no resurrection to life."

Responsorial Psalm
Psalm 98:1, 2–3AB, 3CD–4

R. Lord, when your glory appears, my joy will be full.
Hear, O LORD, a just suit;
attend to my outcry;
hearken to my prayer from lips without deceit. **R.**

My steps have been steadfast in your paths,
my feet have not faltered.
I call upon you, for you will answer me, O God;
incline your ear to me; hear my word. **R.**

Keep me as the apple of your eye,
hide me in the shadow of your wings.
But I in justice shall behold your face;
on waking I shall be content in your presence. **R.**

Second Reading
2 Thessalonians 2:16–3:5
Brothers and sisters:
May our Lord Jesus Christ himself and God our Father,
who has loved us and given us everlasting encouragement
and good hope through his grace,
encourage your hearts and strengthen them in every good deed
and word.
Finally, brothers and sisters, pray for us,
so that the word of the Lord may speed forward and be glorified,
as it did among you,
and that we may be delivered from perverse and wicked people,
for not all have faith.
But the Lord is faithful;
he will strengthen you and guard you from the evil one.
We are confident of you in the Lord that what we instruct you,
you are doing and will continue to do.
May the Lord direct your hearts to the love of God
and to the endurance of Christ.

Gospel
Luke 20:27–38
Some Sadducees, those who deny that there is a resurrection,
came forward and put this question to Jesus, saying,
"Teacher, Moses wrote for us,
If someone's brother dies leaving a wife but no child,

his brother must take the wife
and raise up descendants for his brother.
Now there were seven brothers;
the first married a woman but died childless.
Then the second and the third married her,
and likewise all the seven died childless.
Finally the woman also died.
Now at the resurrection whose wife will that woman be?
For all seven had been married to her."
Jesus said to them,
"The children of this age marry and remarry;
but those who are deemed worthy to attain to the coming age
and to the resurrection of the dead
neither marry nor are given in marriage.
They can no longer die,
for they are like angels;
and they are the children of God
because they are the ones who will rise.
That the dead will rise
even Moses made known in the passage about the bush,
when he called out 'Lord,'
the God of Abraham, the God of Isaac, and the God of Jacob;
and he is not God of the dead, but of the living,
for to him all are alive."

Unmask!

HOMILY GIVEN ON NOVEMBER 10, 2019

There's a show on TV that I watch from time to time called *The Masked Singer*. I don't know if any of you regularly watch *The Masked Singer*, but I really don't quite get the whole concept or why people find it interesting. Basically, actors, athletes, singers, and other famous people dress up in odd costumes and weird outfits. Then they sing individually, and you are supposed to guess who they are. At some point, they begin to give you clues, and they speak to you, but they speak in an altered voice that's a little different so it is not familiar. At the end of the show, the mask is taken off one of the celebrities, and the celebrity is revealed. I know it sounds like I watch this show regularly, but I really don't watch it much at all!

I wonder what masks we wear. You know, we like to figure things out. Perhaps that is the appeal of the show. But I do wonder what masks we wear and if God wants us to be rid of the façade! Maybe one of those masks is we try to show everyone around us "we've got it all together, nothing bothers us, we're strong on our own, we can handle it, and we don't need anybody's help." Could God be asking us to take off that mask and to recognize it is okay to not have it all together? We recognize it is okay for things to bother us. It is okay to not be as strong as we'd like to be because God wants to be there to be our strength. Perhaps this morning each of us can look and ask, "What mask? What mask am I wearing?" God may be encouraging me to remove it!

The first reading said, "Seven brothers with their mother were arrested and tortured with whips and scourges." I don't know whether I'd be brave enough, but I'd like to think I'd be brave enough to withstand the torture. Possibly each of us is sitting there and saying, "Wow, I don't know if I could do that?" Then what does one of the brothers say? "What do you expect to achieve by questioning us?" It's almost as if that brother is saying, "You can do whatever you want, but I'm going to trust in God." I'd like to say that I would be like him. Wouldn't it be wonderful if somehow we can say, "You know, you can do whatever you want to do. Life can throw whatever it's going to throw at me. Whatever situations come, I'll be fine because I know God is with me"? It sounds wonderful, but that is not always easy to do. Maybe that's the mask God wants us to take off, to truly believe that no matter what life throws at us, He is there. After him, the third suffered. He put out his tongue and held out his hands. Again, I don't know if I could stick my tongue out or hold my hands out, not knowing what was going to happen. We don't know what's going to happen today. We don't know what's going to happen tomorrow. **But what we do know is that God wants to be there. He wants to be a part of it. God wants to be our strength, and sharing in His strength is how we can regard our suffering as nothing!** How do we handle our suffering? Do we see value in suffering? When we start to suffer and have difficulties, are we going to walk away from the Lord, or are we going to stick with Him? In many ways and many times, we want to walk away from the Lord. But there's something inside of us saying, "No, I need to stick with the Lord, even in the midst of whatever sufferings and whatever trials."

The psalm says, "Attend to my outcry." What we do know is that God wants to be there, that God hears my cry. But I wonder how many times we want to say to God, "Listen to me! Listen to me! Hear my cry!" Maybe our heart hears the Lord telling us He is listening and we can feel confident He is paying attention because **He is not wearing a mask and He is with us always.** The psalm goes on to say, "Keep me as the apple of Your Eye, hide me in the shadow of Your Wings." One of the masked singers was a person disguised with big wings. Wouldn't it be great to picture ourselves using that image of being hidden in the wings of the Lord? He's got us and is going to hold onto us. "Lord, protect me." And the Lord does want to protect us, but He doesn't always protect us the way we want to be protected. We want to be protected so nothing ever harms us. I think the Lord at times says, "I will protect you when something happens to you. Trust that I am there."

The second reading says, "May our Lord Jesus Christ himself and God our Father, who has loved us and given us everlasting encouragement and good hope through His Grace, encourage your hearts and strengthen them in every good deed and word." May we hear the Lord's encouragement today. May we hear Him speaking to us, that we may be delivered from perverse and wicked people. "He will strengthen you and guard you from the evil one." There's so much stuff out there. We all know it, lots of stuff out there that wants to attack us. Sometimes we put on that mask saying, "I can handle it. I can handle it. I don't need God." **But God wants us to take off that mask and allow Him to walk with us.**

The gospel speaks about the resurrection. The Sadducees didn't believe in the resurrection of the Lord. But Jesus said, "That the dead will rise even Moses made known." There is a resurrection. Are we living as if we believe there is a resurrection? Tomorrow is Veterans Day. Veterans live in a way that supports the belief that there is something greater. That's why they are willing to fight for freedom. Do we believe in something greater? Do we truly believe in the resurrection, and do we live that way? In *The Masked Singer*, the performers hold onto their masks, and the audience must figure out who it is. **God wants us to be unmasked before Him and wants to walk with us and be our strength!**

READINGS FOR NOVEMBER 17, 2019

First Reading
Malachi 3:19–20A
Lo, the day is coming, blazing like an oven,
when all the proud and all evildoers will be stubble,
and the day that is coming will set them on fire,
leaving them neither root nor branch,
says the LORD of hosts.
But for you who fear my name, there will arise
the sun of justice with its healing rays.

Responsorial Psalm
Psalm 98:5–9
R. The Lord comes to rule the earth with justice.
Sing praise to the LORD with the harp,
with the harp and melodious song.
With trumpets and the sound of the horn
sing joyfully before the King, the LORD. **R.**

Let the sea and what fills it resound,
the world and those who dwell in it;
let the rivers clap their hands,
the mountains shout with them for joy. **R.**

Before the LORD, for he comes,
for he comes to rule the earth;
he will rule the world with justice
and the peoples with equity. **R.**

Second Reading
2 Thessalonians 3:7–12
Brothers and sisters:
You know how one must imitate us.
For we did not act in a disorderly way among you,
nor did we eat food received free from anyone.

On the contrary, in toil and drudgery, night and day
we worked, so as not to burden any of you.
Not that we do not have the right.
Rather, we wanted to present ourselves as a model for you,
so that you might imitate us.
In fact, when we were with you,
we instructed you that if anyone was unwilling to work,
neither should that one eat.
We hear that some are conducting themselves among you in a
disorderly way,
by not keeping busy but minding the business of others.
Such people we instruct and urge in the
Lord Jesus Christ to work quietly
and to eat their own food.

Gospel
Luke 21:5–19
While some people were speaking about
how the temple was adorned with costly stones and votive offerings,
Jesus said, "All that you see here–
the days will come when there will not be left
a stone upon another stone that will not be thrown down."
Then they asked him,
"Teacher, when will this happen?
And what sign will there be when all these things are about to happen?"
He answered,
"See that you not be deceived,
for many will come in my name, saying,
'I am he,' and 'The time has come.'
Do not follow them!
When you hear of wars and insurrections,
do not be terrified; for such things must happen first,
but it will not immediately be the end."
Then he said to them,
"Nation will rise against nation, and kingdom against kingdom.
There will be powerful earthquakes, famines, and plagues

from place to place;
and awesome sights and mighty signs will come from the sky."
"Before all this happens, however,
they will seize and persecute you,
they will hand you over to the synagogues and to prisons,
and they will have you led before kings and governors
because of my name.
It will lead to your giving testimony.
Remember, you are not to prepare your defense beforehand,
for I myself shall give you a wisdom in speaking
that all your adversaries will be powerless to resist or refute.
You will even be handed over by parents, brothers, relatives, and friends,
and they will put some of you to death.
You will be hated by all because of my name,
but not a hair on your head will be destroyed.
By your perseverance you will secure your lives."

Making Good Choices

HOMILY GIVEN ON NOVEMBER 17, 2019

My question today is "When was the last time you bought toothpaste? Have you ever gone to a CVS, a Rite Aid, or Walgreens and looked at all the different options there are for toothpaste?" It is almost impossible to find only regular, "good ole" toothpaste! You have to look hard to find it, and then it costs different amounts. It can take a lot of thought. For example, is a certain ingredient worth the additional cost? Will it work as promised? We have so many different choices just when we go to purchase toothpaste!

That is, however, like life. Think of all the choices we have in life, all the decisions we have to make, and all the times we must decide, "Am I going to do this, or am I going to do that?" It can be very confusing, just like the toothpaste aisle. I'm confused! Do I need that additive in my toothpaste or something else? I really don't know what is best for me!

And then there is toothbrush selection! There are available soft, medium, and hard-bristle brushes. I do not know which one I need. Or if you use an electric toothbrush, you should brush for two minutes. How do you brush for two minutes? But we do it!

Of course, the question that comes to mind when making these choices is, "Why do we brush our teeth?" Do we brush our teeth because we are afraid we are going to lose them? Or do we brush our teeth because there is a part of us that thinks we really should brush them if we are going to be around anybody? Just like that question with oral care, we can ask ourselves, "Why do I do the right things in my life? Do I do the right thing in life out of fear of God or out of love for God?" Most of us probably do not brush our teeth because we are afraid that we are going to lose our teeth, but **sometimes we do things in life out of fear of God rather than for love of Him.**

The other night we held a Bible study. We started talking about how we were raised. Some said with a fear of God that was just drilled into you. Other people were raised in a way where the love of God was front and center. If we were raised in a way where the fear of God was pushed into us, maybe it is difficult now to talk to God in any other way than with fear of Him. If we were taught how much God loves us, that is a wonderful thing! But possibly we figured out, "God loves me. I can do whatever I feel like doing." Both teachings are difficult because it could be interpreted either way.

The first reading today said, "But you who fear My name, there will arise the sun of justice with its healing rays." The fear of God can also be, "You are amazing, God, and because you are amazing, I need to recognize that, and I need to respect that." I wonder if we looked at fear of God in that way, if all the choices and all the decisions we would make would try to acknowledge that God is awesome and, as the reading said, make us want to experience "the sun of justice with its healing rays." When it is a warm day and the sun is shining, it feels so good. If it is cold outside and then we feel that heat, it feels so good! It is a wonderful image of God's love coming into us, just as the sunlight's penetrating rays can heal our bodies.

"Lo, the day is coming blazing like an oven when all the proud and all evil doers will be like stubble." It is a good thing that none of us are proud or ever do harmful or evil things (said sarcastically). However, that passage does not mean we have to be afraid. It means **we need to recognize that God does want us to make good choices. He wants us to make good decisions.**

We heard in the psalms today a passage that was very uplifting and incredibly positive and made us feel good. "Sing praise to the Lord." But in the last line, we hear, "He will rule the world with justice and the peoples with equity." **Our God is a just God. He is a God who rules us with justice and love.** He is a God who wants to lead us to make good choices, good decisions. So many times we want justice. If someone harms us, we want justice. It is a good thing that is not the way God distributes justice. How does God supply His justice? He supplies it with love, which does not mean because He loves us, we can do whatever we want to do and poor decisions do not matter.

In the second reading, St. Paul tells us "to imitate us" (the saints). Saints are people we can imitate, people who have gone before us who have put their faith and trust in God. We can see all the different choices that are available, just like the toothpaste aisle, all the different options. The saints chose to follow God. We can look at life in the same way the saints did. Just like the toothpaste aisle, there are so many choices, and in all these different options, we need to make a choice where we are going in life. If we can just say, "God, I am going to go in Your direction," it takes care of itself. In fact, it is written, "we instructed you that, if anyone is unwilling to work, neither should one eat. We hear that some are conducting themselves among you in a disorderly way, by not keeping busy but minding the business of others." It is a good thing that none of us is concerned about the business of others! Maybe, when we heard that passage, we thought to ourselves, *Yeah, look at that person. Look at this person.* But God comes to us with love. He has told us that He loves and cares for us and wants us to look at what we are doing. It is one thing to talk about somebody else because we want to help that person. However, it is another thing to just talk about somebody, "Such people we instruct and urge in the Lord Jesus Christ to work quietly and to eat their own food." Just think about that: work while you eat your own food. Do not worry about anybody else; eat your own food. It sounds like we are talking to a two-year-old, "Eat your own food." **But God wants to be a part of our life. Yes, we need to reach out and help other people when they need to be helped, but do not focus on everybody else and what everybody else is doing wrong.**

In the gospel, we are told, "See that you not be deceived." I wonder what is trying to deceive us right now. We can look at our own hearts and ask, "What is trying to deceive me right now? What is going on in my life that is trying to say that I do not need God, that You just need me?" Then we ask God for the grace not to be deceived and not to follow what is not His will.

"They will seize and persecute you, they will hand you over." It is amazing that people followed Christ in the early days even when He told them that they would be persecuted because they were followers of His. **They followed Him anyway.** The world is full of choices. Just as in the toothpaste aisle, there are tons of choices. Each day we can decide whether we are going to do the right thing out of fear of God or love for Him. **If we choose to do the right things because we love God and we respect Him and thank Him for His gifts, we can ask for the grace to allow Him to help us to make good decisions and good choices.**

READINGS FOR DECEMBER 1, 2019

First Reading
Isaiah 2:1–5
This is what Isaiah, son of Amoz,
saw concerning Judah and Jerusalem.
In days to come,
the mountain of the LORD's house
shall be established as the highest mountain
and raised above the hills.
All nations shall stream toward it;
many peoples shall come and say:
"Come, let us climb the LORD's mountain,
to the house of the God of Jacob,
that he may instruct us in his ways,
and we may walk in his paths."
For from Zion shall go forth instruction,
and the word of the LORD from Jerusalem.
He shall judge between the nations,
and impose terms on many peoples.
They shall beat their swords into plowshares
and their spears into pruning hooks;
one nation shall not raise the sword against another,
nor shall they train for war again.
O house of Jacob, come,
let us walk in the light of the Lord!

Responsorial
Psalm 122: 1–9
R. Let us go rejoicing to the house of the Lord.
I rejoiced because they said to me,
"We will go up to the house of the LORD."
And now we have set foot
within your gates, O Jerusalem. **R.**

Jerusalem, built as a city
with compact unity.
To it the tribes go up,
the tribes of the LORD. **R.**

According to the decree for Israel,
to give thanks to the name of the LORD.
In it are set up judgment seats,
seats for the house of David. **R.**

Pray for the peace of Jerusalem!
May those who love you prosper!
May peace be within your walls,
prosperity in your buildings. **R.**

Because of my brothers and friends
I will say, "Peace be within you!"
Because of the house of the LORD, our God,
I will pray for your good. **R.**

Second Reading
Romans 13:11–14
Brothers and sisters:
You know the time;
it is the hour now for you to awake from sleep.
For our salvation is nearer now than when we first believed;
the night is advanced, the day is at hand.
Let us then throw off the works of darkness
and put on the armor of light;
let us conduct ourselves properly as in the day,
not in orgies and drunkenness,
not in promiscuity and lust,
not in rivalry and jealousy.
But put on the Lord Jesus Christ,
and make no provision for the desires of the flesh.

Gospel

Matthew 24:37–44

Jesus said to his disciples:
"As it was in the days of Noah,
so it will be at the coming of the Son of Man.
In those days before the flood,
they were eating and drinking,
marrying and giving in marriage,
up to the day that Noah entered the ark.
They did not know until the flood came and carried them all away.
So will it be also at the coming of the Son of Man.
Two men will be out in the field;
one will be taken, and one will be left.
Two women will be grinding at the mill;
one will be taken, and one will be left.
Therefore, stay awake!
For you do not know on which day your Lord will come.
Be sure of this: if the master of the house
had known the hour of night when the thief was coming,
he would have stayed awake
and not let his house be broken into.
So too, you also must be prepared,
for at an hour you do not expect, the Son of Man will come."

Stay Awake

HOMILY GIVEN ON DECEMBER 1, 2019

You may have noticed the tree standing to the side of the altar. I want to start off by saying it was donated; we did not spend a dime for that tree. It was donated to me in my last parish about seven years ago, but this year, they were not able to use it anymore. I was then asked if I would like the tree, and I thought to myself, *Where am I going to put it?* So I brought it here and looked around and decided to put it in this corner. It is an Advent tree, not an ordinary Christmas tree, but an Advent tree. You can see the streamers of two purple, then a rose, and then a purple again. It has lights on it that will not be lit until Christmas arrives, but it does look very good when the lights are lit. My hope is that you will just look at it as you do our Advent wreath so, when we come into church over the next several weeks, we will be able to look at that tree and be reminded that Advent is a time of preparation.

Advent is a time when we prepare for the coming of Christ at Christmas, when we celebrate the birth of Jesus and prepare for His coming again at the end of time. When we look at the tree, we can ask ourselves, "How am I preparing? This Advent, am I going to do anything differently? This Advent, am I going to try to change? Am I going to realize that I am preparing, not just for the coming of Christ and remembering Him as a baby, but also to remember that one day He is going to come a second time? When He comes a second time, am I going to be with Him?" This is an opportunity for us to say, "How do I prepare to be with Christ?"

All of us just celebrated Thanksgiving in one way or another, and while the cooking and eating are important, the preparation is probably the most important part of the meal. None of us wants to eat a raw turkey! We need to make sure everything is cooked and comes out of the oven at the right time. There is a lot of preparation needed in making a big dinner. So many times we just move through life and do not really think too much about it, the preparation. Advent is a time for us to step back and to think about what we really need beyond just this very moment. We need to look and see how we are living and perhaps what we can do differently.

I did not see the entire Macy's parade, but I did see footage of the balloons that were extremely high off the ground. The handlers were preparing for high winds, which did occur, and almost jeopardized whether the balloons could be carried along the parade route. In the end, the parade went on as usual, but those people holding the balloons had to be prepared because they did not know which way the wind was going to be pulling them, and that's what happens to us too. **We do not know where life is going to be pulling us. The gospel says, "Stay awake." We need to be prepared.**

One of the ways we can prepare to stay awake throughout the day is by sleeping at night. Similarly, if we live each day remembering that the Lord is there, then, when we are being pulled in all different directions, we can rely on our relationship with Him. To keep our relationship with God, we need to be sure we pray each day. We need to talk to God every day or at least invite Him in every day. If we are already doing that, wonderful. Perhaps we can do it just a little bit longer.

What will we do differently this year? In reflecting on the people in the days before the flood, they were eating, drinking, marrying, and sharing in marriage, but not taking care of what they had. They were not necessarily taking care of their relationship with God. That can remind us to change our focus, from taking care of so many different things that, in doing so, we neglect to take care of our relationship with God also. "So will it be also at the coming of the Son of Man. Two men will be out in the field; one will be taken and one will be left." We need to stay awake, "For you do not know on which day your Lord will come." It does not mean we have to live in fear. It just means we must be alert. **We want to be with the Lord**

when He comes again, and we will be with Him if we live our lives in His way. We can "stay awake" by being prepared and paying attention.

The second reading said, "You know the time; it is the hour now for you to wake from sleep." We all know the time that would be best for us. We know how it is best to talk and deal with situations. We basically know, if we ask God to give us advice about what to do, we can almost predict what He is going to say. Of course, some decisions are more difficult than others, but for the most part, we know what God might say. We just need to ask God for the grace and strength to do what we know is best for us.

We are told, "Let us throw off the works of darkness and put on the armor of light." We need to put on the Lord Jesus Christ many times each day. Do we hear that we need to put on the "armor of light"? The Advent tree has little lights on it. When Christmas comes and it is lit, the light on the tree represents the Light of Christ coming into the world. We could decide right now to put on the armor of light. What a wonderful image! What are we doing right now in our lives? Things that just lead us to more darkness than to light? "Let us conduct ourselves properly, not in orgies and drunkenness," promiscuity, lust, rivalry, and jealousy. What can we do differently?

The psalm said, "Let us go rejoicing to the House of the Lord." The House of the Lord is heaven, eternity. Let us go rejoicing there. Are we preparing ourselves to go rejoicing there? The psalm also said, "May peace be within your walls." Peace, perhaps that is what we want this Advent. Maybe we could just invite God's peace within us and pray, "Lord, during this busy time, may You give me Your peace."

In the first reading, "The mountain of the Lord's House shall be established as the highest mountain." That is another great image, the mountain of the Lord's House. That's what we await. That is what we look forward to and pray that "He may instruct us in His Ways." That is the hardest part. God wants to instruct us in His ways, but we do not always want to listen. The last line of the first reading, "let us walk in the Light of the Lord."

So how are we going to prepare ourselves this Advent? May we put on the "armor of light" and allow the Lord to dwell deep within us. We all experienced Thanksgiving dinner in different ways, but it always requires preparation. **We all want to experience eternal life, but preparation**

needs to go into that as well. Today, we ask for the grace to allow the Lord deep within us, to allow His light deep within so we can have the courage we need to change where we may need to change and to do things differently where we may need to do things differently.

As we prepare for the coming of the Lord, let us allow His light deep within us!

READINGS FOR DECEMBER 15, 2019

First Reading
Isaiah 35:1–6A, 10

The desert and the parched land will exult;
the steppe will rejoice and bloom.
They will bloom with abundant flowers,
and rejoice with joyful song.
The glory of Lebanon will be given to them,
the splendor of Carmel and Sharon;
they will see the glory of the LORD,
the splendor of our God.
Strengthen the hands that are feeble,
make firm the knees that are weak,
say to those whose hearts are frightened:
Be strong, fear not!
Here is your God,
he comes with vindication;
with divine recompense
he comes to save you.
Then will the eyes of the blind be opened,
the ears of the deaf be cleared;
then will the lame leap like a stag,
then the tongue of the mute will sing.
Those whom the LORD has ransomed will return
and enter Zion singing,
crowned with everlasting joy;
they will meet with joy and gladness,
sorrow and mourning will flee.

Responsorial Psalm
Psalm 146:6–10
R. Lord, come and save us.
or:
R. Alleluia.
The LORD God keeps faith forever,

secures justice for the oppressed,
gives food to the hungry.
The LORD sets captives free. **R.**

The LORD gives sight to the blind;
the LORD raises up those who were bowed down.
The LORD loves the just;
the LORD protects strangers. **R.**

The fatherless and the widow he sustains,
but the way of the wicked he thwarts.
The LORD shall reign forever;
your God, O Zion, through all generations. **R.**

Second Reading
James 5:7–10
Be patient, brothers and sisters,
until the coming of the Lord.
See how the farmer waits for the precious fruit of the earth,
being patient with it
until it receives the early and the late rains.
You too must be patient.
Make your hearts firm,
because the coming of the Lord is at hand.
Do not complain, brothers and sisters, about one another,
that you may not be judged.
Behold, the Judge is standing before the gates.
Take as an example of hardship and patience, brothers and sisters,
the prophets who spoke in the name of the Lord.

Gospel
Matthew 11:2–11
When John the Baptist heard in prison of the works of the Christ,
he sent his disciples to Jesus with this question,
"Are you the one who is to come,
or should we look for another?"

Jesus said to them in reply,
"Go and tell John what you hear and see:
the blind regain their sight,
the lame walk,
lepers are cleansed,
the deaf hear,
the dead are raised,
and the poor have the good news proclaimed to them.
And blessed is the one who takes no offense at me."

As they were going off,
Jesus began to speak to the crowds about John,
"What did you go out to the desert to see?
A reed swayed by the wind?
Then what did you go out to see?
Someone dressed in fine clothing?
Those who wear fine clothing are in royal palaces.
Then why did you go out? To see a prophet?
Yes, I tell you, and more than a prophet.
This is the one about whom it is written:
Behold, I am sending my messenger ahead of you;
he will prepare your way before you.
Amen, I say to you,
among those born of women
there has been none greater than John the Baptist;
yet the least in the kingdom of heaven is greater than he."

God's Time

HOMILY GIVEN DECEMBER 15, 2019

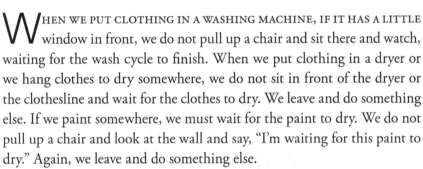

When we put clothing in a washing machine, if it has a little window in front, we do not pull up a chair and sit there and watch, waiting for the wash cycle to finish. When we put clothing in a dryer or we hang clothes to dry somewhere, we do not sit in front of the dryer or the clothesline and wait for the clothes to dry. We leave and do something else. If we paint somewhere, we must wait for the paint to dry. We do not pull up a chair and look at the wall and say, "I'm waiting for this paint to dry." Again, we leave and do something else.

The second reading talked about being patient. One of the ways we are patient is we do not just sit and wait for something to happen. We go about our lives. We do different things. However, when it comes to things that we want God to do for us, many times we just want to tell God, "When are You going to do this?" Just as we would not look at a washing machine and wait for the clothes to be washed, we do not need to watch and wait with God. We are called to live our lives and to trust that God is present.

This weekend some of our teenagers are at a Kairos retreat. "Kairos" means "in God's time." Patience means we try to live in God's time. This is the third Sunday of Advent, Gaudete Sunday, when we celebrate God and rejoice for the Lord is near. I wear rose vestments. **When we make the conscious decision to live in God's time, then we can be patient and live in joy.** When we focus on our time and how and when we want things done, for the most part, we are not going to experience the same joy.

The second reading also spoke about a farmer and explained how the farmer waits for the precious fruit of the earth and is patiently waiting for the early and late rains. A farmer does not pull up a chair and look at his field and just sit there and wait. Rather he keeps doing what he needs to do. Today, we pray that God gives us the strength to keep doing what we need to do and to somehow be patient and joyful during our waiting. We need to somehow trust in God's time. We need to "Make your hearts firm … Do not complain, brothers and sisters, about one another …"

Do not complain about one another. I wonder if we may have already done that today once, twice, or even three times, complain about somebody. Can we live in God's time? If so, then we can be joyful. When somebody isn't quite doing things the way we would like them to or when someone might be distracting us in some way, we can say, "Okay, God, I'm living in Your time here. You help me with this situation. You help me with this person."

The gospel said, "What did you go out to the desert to see?" referring to looking for John the Baptist. What did you go out to see? Why did you go out? Maybe today we ask ourselves, "Why am I here? What did I come here to see?" Did we come here to experience God's grace in some way? Did we come here because someone said, "Get in the car. You are coming to church"? Did we come here today because, for some reason, we know that, if we place ourselves in God's presence, no matter whatever else is going on in our lives, we will be able to experience His joy? Today, as we leave Mass, we can decide whether we are going to live in our time or in God's time.

The gospel continues, "There has been none greater than John the Baptist; yet the least in the kingdom of heaven is greater than he." This means each one of us is greater than the greatest person that Jesus points out, which is John the Baptist. Perhaps that is a reason we can live in joy. Maybe we sit here and say, "Father Dan, you don't know my life. If you knew my life, you would know that there is no way I can live in joy!" We **can** live in joy, and we **can** be patient **if we strive to live in God's time!**

The first reading said, "Strengthen the hands that are feeble, make firm the knees that are weak, say to those whose hearts are frightened: Be strong, fear not! Here is your God." "Here is your God" and not just here in this church, but here is our God, in each one of us, here is our God! If we could only remember that, then we could live in joy. Yes, all kinds of situations happen. All kinds of situations happen in our church and in our world. If somehow, we can remember, "Here is your God," then we can experience His joy.

Just as when we are washing clothes, we do not sit down and watch the washer working but continue with our lives. We do not watch clothes drying, and we do not watch paint dry. The farmer does not watch his field grow but continues to move on to other chores. **We too can continue to move on, trusting God and being patient. If we strive to live in God's time,** we **can** do that! We can experience His joy if we remember, "Here is our God. He is right here." (Fr. Dan taps his chest.) When we do that and we do that no matter what is happening in our lives, we can be joyful people. **Ultimately the choice is ours. We need to remember to live in God's time, not ours. When we live in God's time, the joy can be amazing!**

READINGS FOR DECEMBER 22, 2019

First Reading
Isaiah 7:10–14
The LORD spoke to Ahaz, saying:
Ask for a sign from the LORD, your God;
let it be deep as the netherworld, or high as the sky!
But Ahaz answered,
"I will not ask! I will not tempt the LORD!"
Then Isaiah said:
Listen, O house of David!
Is it not enough for you to weary people,
must you also weary my God?
Therefore the Lord himself will give you this sign:
the virgin shall conceive, and bear a son,
and shall name him Emmanuel.

Responsorial Psalm
Psalm 24:1–6
R. Let the Lord enter; he is king of glory.
The LORD's are the earth and its fullness;
the world and those who dwell in it.
For he founded it upon the seas
and established it upon the rivers. **R.**

Who can ascend the mountain of the LORD?
or who may stand in his holy place?
One whose hands are sinless, whose heart is clean,
who desires not what is vain. **R.**

He shall receive a blessing from the LORD,
a reward from God his savior.
Such is the race that seeks for him,
that seeks the face of the God of Jacob. **R.**

Second Reading
Romans 1:1–7
Paul, a slave of Christ Jesus,
called to be an apostle and set apart for the gospel of God,
which he promised previously through his
prophets in the holy Scriptures,
the gospel about his Son, descended from David according to the flesh,
but established as Son of God in power
according to the Spirit of holiness
through resurrection from the dead, Jesus Christ our Lord.
Through him we have received the grace of apostleship,
to bring about the obedience of faith,
for the sake of his name, among all the Gentiles,
among whom are you also, who are called to belong to Jesus Christ;
to all the beloved of God in Rome, called to be holy.
Grace to you and peace from God our Father
and the Lord Jesus Christ.

Gospel
Matthew 1:18–24
This is how the birth of Jesus Christ came about.
When his mother Mary was betrothed to Joseph,
but before they lived together,
she was found with child through the Holy Spirit.
Joseph her husband, since he was a righteous man,
yet unwilling to expose her to shame,
decided to divorce her quietly.
Such was his intention when, behold,
the angel of the Lord appeared to him in a dream and said,
"Joseph, son of David,
do not be afraid to take Mary your wife into your home.
For it is through the Holy Spirit
that this child has been conceived in her.
She will bear a son and you are to name him Jesus,
because he will save his people from their sins."
All this took place to fulfill what the Lord had said through the prophet:

Behold, the virgin shall conceive and bear a son,
and they shall name him Emmanuel,
which means "God is with us."
When Joseph awoke,
he did as the angel of the Lord had commanded him
and took his wife into his home.

God Is with Us

HOMILY GIVEN DECEMBER 22, 2019

We find ourselves today, on this fourth Sunday of Advent, in limbo, almost in between because Christmas is close. I am still wearing purple, but the Christmas trees are up. The wreaths are hanging, and there is some white here and there. The trees are up, but they are not lit yet, because it is still not Christmas. Our Advent wreath is here, right next to the manger scene. So in this limbo state, we are not exactly sure whether we should start celebrating Christmas or wait a couple of days to begin our Christmas festivities.

Many have already started celebrating. Family is coming into town, and different things are happening due to the proximity of Christmas. Many times in our lives, we can find ourselves in a state of feeling like we are in between. We are in limbo. We are not exactly sure what we are supposed to do next or where we are supposed to be next. Maybe sometimes we are in limbo when it comes to good and bad, good and evil. Perhaps somewhere inside of us, we are feeling, "This is not so bad. If I do this, it really is not so bad" or "I know we are supposed to be good. But what does it really mean to be good, and how good do I have to be to be good, or how bad do I have to be to be bad?"

We look at different things, and we think about different situations and find ourselves in places we do not anticipate. And in this season, when we do not always eat the way we should, we say to ourselves, "What's the difference between being healthy and unhealthy, and how healthy do I need to be? Can I be sort of healthy. Do I need to be really healthy, and how unhealthy can I become? Can I do a little bit of stuff that I should not be doing when it comes to my body, food, or exercise, or do I really need to try to be as healthy as I can be?" We feel in limbo.

However, the Lord Jesus Christ came into our world to help us, especially during these in-between times. And then there are those times when we feel like we are not exactly sure which direction we should go, how good we should be, or how healthy we should try to be.

The first reading said the Lord spoke to Ahaz. "Ask for a sign from the LORD, your God." And Ahaz responds, "I will not ask!" It is not because he does not really want to ask for a sign. He has not asked for a sign, not because he doesn't want to tempt God, but because, if he asked God for a sign and God gave him that sign, then he might just have to do what God is asking of him. So if he does not ask for the sign, he does not have to deal with it at all.

In life, there are so many times we are happy that God does not give us signs. "God, if I just stay quiet, I could do what I want to do, and I won't have to worry about it." And then there are times when we get mad at God because we asked for a sign and He doesn't give it to us. Then we say, "Okay, God, I know before I didn't want the sign, but right now I want the sign. So give me a sign right now!"

Signs can be good things sometimes, as in, "Do not enter, turn here, or stop." Perhaps each of us can investigate our own hearts and ask ourselves, "Is God trying to give me a sign and I'm not paying attention? Is God showing me His presence, but I would rather not see it?" And then other times, I am asking God for a sign, and I feel like He is not doing anything. Maybe the problem is that **He's giving me a sign but not the sign I want to receive.**

The psalmist asks, "Let the Lord enter." **Let the Lord enter. Christmas and Advent are all about letting the Lord enter.** But asking for a sign can be a risk, as can letting the Lord enter be a risk. Think about it today, right now. If we said, "Lord, enter. Enter inside of me," what is that going to mean? What is that going to mean in the parking lot? What is it going to mean in the store later today? What is that going to mean whatever we're doing over the next few days? If I "let the Lord enter," St. Paul says we will be "a slave of Christ." A slave is one who does what the master says, and slavery has an unbelievably bad connotation unless we are willing to be slaves of Christ; we are willing to do what our Master asks us to do. But again, there's risk. There's a risk if I say, "Okay, Lord, whatever you ask of me, I will do." Paul goes on to say that we have received "the grace of apostleship." A disciple sits at the feet of the Master, and an apostle then goes out and shares what he learns from the Master.

It does not mean we have to go out and say all these unusual things. It just means we go out and try to live, remembering that we let the Lord enter inside of us. And when we do that, we are an apostle because we are showing Christ to others. We are called to be holy. I should ask God to help me to be holy. Holy? If I ask God to help me to be holy, what is that going to mean? Maybe I will ask God to be half holy or three-quarters holy. But I am not sure I want to ask God to be totally holy. If I ask God to be holy, I may have to listen to Him a little bit more. I will have to follow His guidance a little bit more. I may have to let go of my will a little bit and ask Him what His will is!

In the gospel, Mary was found to be with child through the Holy Spirit. Mary's yes is a big yes, but St. Joseph's yes was a big yes too because he was not the one who was with child. He had to trust that everything he was being told was the truth. Mary knew it was the truth. Joseph had to trust. **Today we pray that we will be able to trust that all we have heard about God, that He wants to be a part of our lives and that He came into this world to save us, is true.** "Do not be afraid, … name him 'Emmanuel, which means, 'God is with us.'" Do not be afraid. God is with us.

Perhaps that is the phrase we leave with today. **Do not be afraid. God is with us.** So we find ourselves in this in-between time. Decorations are up, trees are out but not lit, and purple is still prevalent because it is Advent, but it is almost Christmas. In life, we find ourselves today and, many times, in limbo.

May we be not afraid. May we truly trust that God is with us.

READINGS FOR DECEMBER 29, 2019

First Reading
Sirach 3:2–6, 12–14
God sets a father in honor over his children;
a mother's authority he confirms over her sons.
Whoever honors his father atones for sins,
and preserves himself from them.
When he prays, he is heard;
he stores up riches who reveres his mother.
Whoever honors his father is gladdened by children,
and, when he prays, is heard.
Whoever reveres his father will live a long life;
he who obeys his father brings comfort to his mother.
My son, take care of your father when he is old;
grieve him not as long as he lives.
Even if his mind fail, be considerate of him;
revile him not all the days of his life;
kindness to a father will not be forgotten,
firmly planted against the debt of your sins
—a house raised in justice to you.

Responsorial Psalm
Psalm 128:1–5
R. Blessed are those who fear the Lord and walk in his ways.
Blessed is everyone who fears the LORD,
who walks in his ways!
For you shall eat the fruit of your handiwork;
blessed shall you be, and favored. **R.**

Your wife shall be like a fruitful vine
in the recesses of your home;
your children like olive plants
around your table. **R.**

Behold, thus is the man blessed
who fears the LORD.

The LORD bless you from Zion:
may you see the prosperity of Jerusalem
all the days of your life. **R.**

Second Reading
Colossians 3:12–21
Brothers and sisters:
Put on, as God's chosen ones, holy and beloved,
heartfelt compassion, kindness, humility, gentleness, and patience,
bearing with one another and forgiving one another,
if one has a grievance against another;
as the Lord has forgiven you, so must you also do.
And over all these put on love,
that is, the bond of perfection.
And let the peace of Christ control your hearts,
the peace into which you were also called in one body.
And be thankful.
Let the word of Christ dwell in you richly,
as in all wisdom you teach and admonish one another,
singing psalms, hymns, and spiritual songs
with gratitude in your hearts to God.
And whatever you do, in word or in deed,
do everything in the name of the Lord Jesus,
giving thanks to God the Father through him.
Wives, be subordinate to your husbands, as is proper in the Lord.
Husbands, love your wives and avoid any bitterness toward them.
Children, obey your parents in everything
for this is pleasing to the Lord.
Fathers, do not provoke your children so they
may not become discouraged.

Gospel
Matthew 2:13–15, 19–23
When the magi had departed, behold,
the angel of the Lord appeared to Joseph in a dream and said,
"Rise, take the child and his mother, flee to Egypt,

and stay there until I tell you.
Herod is going to search for the child to destroy him."
Joseph rose and took the child and his mother by night
and departed for Egypt.
He stayed there until the death of Herod,
that what the Lord had said through the prophet might be fulfilled,
Out of Egypt I called my son.

When Herod had died, behold,
the angel of the Lord appeared in a dream
to Joseph in Egypt and said,
"Rise, take the child and his mother and go to the land of Israel,
for those who sought the child's life are dead."
He rose, took the child and his mother,
and went to the land of Israel.
But when he heard that Archelaus was ruling over Judea
in place of his father Herod,
he was afraid to go back there.
And because he had been warned in a dream,
he departed for the region of Galilee.
He went and dwelt in a town called Nazareth,
so that what had been spoken through the prophets
might be fulfilled,
He shall be called a Nazorean.

Families

HOMILY GIVEN ON DECEMBER 29, 2019

Many of us get together on Christmas with family and friends, and for some, that is a good experience, but for others, it might be a more difficult experience. However, most of us get together as a family, and we pray that God can be present during our family time. I have five nieces, and they decided that they were going to have a gingerbread house contest. Three of them were on one team and two on the other, and three of us were judges: my brother-in-law, my brother, and me. The judges did not know whose house was whose.

When the time came for the houses to be judged, the judges went to the room to view the houses. One was quite simple but a genuinely nice gingerbread house. The other one was, shall we say, creative and a little strange or odd. I will not go into what made it odd or strange, but it was both those adjectives! The creators of this house had decided beforehand that they knew that they would have at least my vote because it was so odd and strange. According to their strategy, all they had to do was get the vote of one of the other judges to win. However, they did not win because the other judges voted for the simple house that was kind of boring, the plain gingerbread house.

Another thing our family did was pass around party favors. With the ones we had, you could pull the end, and a prize would emerge from it. The prize that came out of these tubes was a paper crown. So, the entire evening we waited to see who could keep their crown on their head the longest, and that person would be the winner of the game. No one won anything except bragging rights for keeping the crown on the longest. But the next morning, my niece came downstairs, and she still had her crown on! When we texted my sister, who had left the house the night before, to tell her who the winner was, she stunned us by saying she still had her crown on too! What was the point!? I don't know. Maybe they are still wearing those silly paper crowns! Probably all of us have stories related to our families: some we can tell and maybe others we cannot or should not.

We gather here tonight as a church family on this Feast of the Holy Family: Jesus, Mary, and Joseph. As a church family, we can tell stories: some of these stories are good, and others are a little more difficult. Just as we are called to support one another in our own families through the good and the difficult times, we pray that God will bless not just our individual families, but our church family also. We are brothers and sisters in Christ; we will support one another and strengthen one another because the center of our church family is what we do right here. **If somehow the Eucharist, the body of Christ, can be the center of our individual families, then we are able to live in a family that can be holy. Our families could somehow follow the ways of God.**

In the first reading, we are told, "God sets a father in honor over his children; a mother's authority He confirms over her sons." We know we are supposed to honor our mother and father, but sometimes we decide whether we think they deserve our honor. Now sometimes we may think, *I know I'm **supposed** to honor them.* Maybe some of us here today have a difficult relationship with our mother and/or father. Perhaps tonight we can ask God for the grace to honor them and to pray for them and place them in His hands. **Perhaps as we gather here tonight and for whatever reason, we are having a difficult relationship with a mother or a father. Right now, we can place that situation in God's hands.** "My son, take care of your father when he is old ... even if his mind fail, be considerate of him ... Kindness to a father will not be forgotten ..."

I wonder where God might be asking us to be kind to a father, a mother, a brother, or a sister. Maybe we are finding it difficult. Perhaps there are stories we just cannot forget, situations we cannot let go. Tonight, in a real sense, we place our families in God's hands. **Perhaps we can say,**

"God, help me to want to have a better relationship with my family. Help me to want to forgive."

The psalm said, "For you shall eat the fruit of your handiwork." How we treat others is sometimes how others treat us, but not always. Sometimes we treat others with love, respect, and honor, and we are not treated in that same way. In those times, we must stop and say that God still wants us to treat those people with love, respect, and honor.

The second reading said, "Put on, as God's chosen ones, Holy and Beloved, heartfelt compassion, kindness, humility, gentleness, patience, bearing with one another and forgiving one another; **if one has a grievance against another, as the Lord has forgiven you, so must you also do."** What if we all were to hang that Bible passage somewhere in our homes? If we put it on the refrigerator, every day we could ask God to help us pick one fruit of the Holy Spirit: compassion, kindness, humility, gentleness, patience, or forgiveness. The fruits of the Spirit defined the Holy Family. We would expect nothing else, but choosing to use them as a model for us to follow is something which we can and should always strive toward. We may not always succeed, but it is a wonderful goal!

And then there is that perfect part that we love, "Wives, be subordinate to your husbands." Sometimes we forget the next line that is connected to the first and cannot be separated from it, "Husbands, love your wives … Children, obey your parents … Fathers, do not provoke your children." **That reading is telling us all to work together; we should work together in our family and support one another.**

"The angel of the Lord appeared to Joseph in a dream and said …" He told Joseph what he needed to do. Joseph strove to take care of his family. We are all God's children, and as God's children, He wants to take care of His family. **Can we take the chance and let Him take control and oversee our lives? Can we take the chance and strive to show honor and respect even when it is exceedingly difficult?**

We all have stories in our families. Sometimes those stories are wonderful ones, and other times they are more difficult. **Tonight, may we allow the Lord to enter our stories and truly allow Him to be the center of all that we are: the center of our families!**

READINGS FOR JANUARY 12, 2020

First Reading
Isaiah 42:1–4, 6–7
Thus says the LORD:
Here is my servant whom I uphold,
my chosen one with whom I am pleased,
upon whom I have put my spirit;
he shall bring forth justice to the nations,
not crying out, not shouting,
not making his voice heard in the street.
A bruised reed he shall not break,
and a smoldering wick he shall not quench,
until he establishes justice on the earth;
the coastlands will wait for his teaching.
I, the LORD, have called you for the victory of justice,
I have grasped you by the hand;
I formed you, and set you
as a covenant of the people,
a light for the nations,
to open the eyes of the blind,
to bring out prisoners from confinement,
and from the dungeon, those who live in darkness.

Responsorial Psalm
Psalms 29:1–4, 9–10
R. The Lord will bless his people with peace.
Give to the LORD, you sons of God,
give to the LORD glory and praise,
give to the LORD the glory due his name;
adore the LORD in holy attire. **R.**

The voice of the LORD is over the waters,
the LORD, over vast waters.
The voice of the LORD is mighty;
the voice of the LORD is majestic. **R.**

The God of glory thunders,
and in his temple all say, "Glory!"
The LORD is enthroned above the flood;
the LORD is enthroned as king forever. **R.**

Second Reading
Acts 10:34–38
Peter proceeded to speak to those gathered
in the house of Cornelius, saying:
"In truth, I see that God shows no partiality.
Rather, in every nation whoever fears him and acts uprightly
is acceptable to him.
You know the word that he sent to the Israelites
as he proclaimed peace through Jesus Christ, who is Lord of all,
what has happened all over Judea,
beginning in Galilee after the baptism
that John preached,
how God anointed Jesus of Nazareth
with the Holy Spirit and power.
He went about doing good
and healing all those oppressed by the devil,
for God was with him."

Gospel
Matthew 3:13–17
Jesus came from Galilee to John at the Jordan
to be baptized by him.
John tried to prevent him, saying,
"I need to be baptized by you,
and yet you are coming to me?"
Jesus said to him in reply,
"Allow it now, for thus it is fitting for us
to fulfill all righteousness."
Then he allowed him.
After Jesus was baptized,
he came up from the water and behold,

the heavens were opened for him,
and he saw the Spirit of God descending like a dove
and coming upon him.
And a voice came from the heavens, saying,
"This is my beloved Son, with whom I am well pleased."

The Face of Jesus

HOMILY GIVEN ON JANUARY 12, 2020

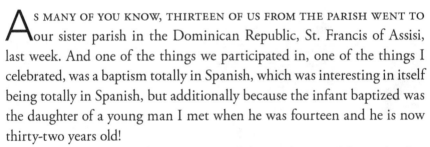

As many of you know, thirteen of us from the parish went to our sister parish in the Dominican Republic, St. Francis of Assisi, last week. And one of the things we participated in, one of the things I celebrated, was a baptism totally in Spanish, which was interesting in itself being totally in Spanish, but additionally because the infant baptized was the daughter of a young man I met when he was fourteen and he is now thirty-two years old!

Today is the Feast of the Baptism of the Lord. We celebrate the fact that we were baptized into the Lord's life, death, and resurrection, and being baptized into the life, death, and resurrection of Jesus means that we try to live our lives as Jesus would have us. So during the baptism in Spanish, there were a couple spots where the language barrier caused a slight problem. For example, there is a word *tomo*. If you say it one way, you are saying, "Jesus took the children to Himself." If you say it another way, you are saying, "I drank the children." Unfortunately I pronounced it the way that it meant, "I drank the children." Luckily, everybody knew what I meant! There is another word that is *Papas*. Pronounced one way, it means "potato," and another way, it means "parents." Again, said incorrectly, you ask the potatoes if they are going to uphold their duties as parents of these children!

However, for the most part, the service went well, and as you know, it is amazing that our faith is our faith, whether we are here in the United

States or the Dominican Republic, whether we have lots of gifts or not much materially at all. Our faith is still our faith. **We transported twenty-four fifty-pound bags of donations, twenty-four fifty-pound bags!** You should have seen the vehicle and the airport when we got out onto the tarmac there, but everything was fairly easily handled. We also took the monetary donations that you gave us. Thank you to all who gave in that way or in any way toward the success of this trip!

One day we painted a school. I have this problem when it comes to ladders. I've talked about that before during Advent, when I tried to go up a ladder to decorate the big tree in the church. In the Dominican Republic, there was not a ladder that I really could use. So I did one of my "ladder things," that is, I used a makeshift ladder again. I did not fall off it, but I almost did! My ladder was a table with a desk on top of the table. I was standing on the desk that was on top of the table, but I got to where I needed to go! We figure things out, but in truth, that is where God comes in. There are times when we think we just cannot reach that spot. We think, *I just don't know what I'm going to do in that situation*. But when we allow God to be a part of the situation and the solution, then we might just be able to figure out something even though we are not so sure how to accomplish it!

We also worked with children. We went to different churches and helped the children with arts and crafts and did some singing. We took 150 pounds of tennis balls, or about 1,200 tennis balls. You might think, *A tennis ball? That is hardly a gift for somebody*. You might think a tennis ball would not be a big deal, but you should have seen the faces of the children who received a tennis ball! Some of us had the opportunity to toss them tennis balls and watch while they were bouncing it, and the simple joy on their faces was just wonderful.

There was one young man who was wearing a yellow shirt, and he just stood out to me. We were driving, and he was waiting for us. He was just shaking so much because he knew he was getting something. He did not know what he was getting. **We gave him a simple tennis ball, and he was just so thrilled, so happy! I wonder how many things God has given to us, simple things, and we do not realize just how special those things are. Maybe tonight is an opportunity for us to stop and think about the simple things God has given to me and possibly I take for**

granted. Perhaps one of the simplest things is our faith itself. God has given us Himself, hardly a simple thing, but something, at times, we take for granted.

We also brought two big duffle bags of glasses, reading glasses for the most part. You would have thought we were giving out gold with those glasses while we simply drive to the store and purchase them. Those of us who were helping with the glasses became quite good at it. People just kept coming looking for glasses, and it was amazing to see their faces. I wonder how many times God tries to show Himself to us? We just do not see Him.

A missionary nun, Sister Lisa, oversaw the group and asked how we were doing each night. We would say evening prayer, and sometimes evening prayer was 11:00 p.m. or midnight. We were so tired, but when she asked us, "Where did you see the face of Jesus?" even though we were very tired, every person responded where, and sometimes the answers were longer than we may have wanted them to be at that hour. I wonder if we did that every night before we went to bed, to ask ourselves, **"Where did I see the face of Jesus today?" If we took that simple moment, I bet we would start to discover that we see the face of Jesus a lot more often than we realize!**

The first reading said, "my chosen one with whom I am well pleased." That line is repeated in the gospel, "This is my Beloved Son, with whom I am well pleased." I would suggest that most of us probably want God to be well pleased with us. How does that happen? Well, "I have grasped you by the hand; I have formed you." That is what God said, "I have grasped you by the hand." How can we be pleasing to God? How can we live out our baptismal promises? We simply can do that by holding the Lord's hand. **The Lord wants to be our light, and He is the "Light for the Nations." No matter where we live, no matter what part of the world we live in, He wants to be "a Light for the Nations," and He wants to be a light for each one of us. We simply can ask God each day to be our light.**

Then in the psalm, "Give to the Lord," we might think of what we might give to the Lord. We could give Him the gift of ourselves. What if we said every day, "Lord, I give You myself today"? The reading in the psalm went on to refer to "the Voice of the Lord." The Lord simply wants us to listen to Him. Maybe tonight we can ask ourselves, "Am I really listening, or am I listening for what I want to hear?" The psalm also says,

"The God of Glory Thunders." We know there have been earthquakes in Puerto Rico, and one morning at about 4:00 a.m., some thought they felt an earthquake. And they did, but it was in Puerto Rico, not the Dominican Republic. I did not feel it because it was early morning and I was dead tired and still asleep! I wonder how many times the Lord thunders like that earthquake. He thunders, and we do not hear Him because we are asleep. Maybe **we can reflect on our lives, "Is God trying to thunder His voice to me? Has God been trying to reach out to me and I'm just not paying attention?"**

The second reading said, "In truth, I see that God shows no partiality." When we were in the Dominican Republic, there were times I thought to myself, *I wonder does God show partiality? I have so much, and they have so little.* Then I stopped and thought, *Or is God showing partiality to those who have little because, when you have less, there is not as much in the way when you are trying to be a person of faith?* The reality is that God does not show people partiality. We just are all different.

In the gospel, we heard that Jesus was baptized, "This is My Beloved Son." One person on the trip asked, "How long does it take before you stop feeling guilty for all you have compared to the people in the Dominican Republic?"

To me, that was an interesting statement. I responded, "You don't need to feel guilty. It is what it is. We are here, other people are other places, and we all have different things."

We are all blessed in different ways. Perhaps the best thing we can do is try to see the face of Jesus in someone we meet today. When we do that, we are living out our baptismal promises when we were baptized into the life, death, and resurrection of Jesus.

May God give us the grace to see the face of Jesus each day. When we do that, we do not have to feel guilty because then we will know what we are to say, what we are to do, and what we are to see.

READINGS FOR JANUARY 19, 2020

First Reading
Isaiah 49:3, 5–6

The LORD said to me: You are my servant,
Israel, through whom I show my glory.
Now the LORD has spoken
who formed me as his servant from the womb,
that Jacob may be brought back to him
and Israel gathered to him;
and I am made glorious in the sight of the LORD,
and my God is now my strength!
It is too little, the LORD says, for you to be my servant,
to raise up the tribes of Jacob,
and restore the survivors of Israel;
I will make you a light to the nations,
that my salvation may reach to the ends of the earth.

Responsorial Psalm
Psalm 40:2, 4, 7–10

R. Here am I, Lord; I come to do your will.
I have waited, waited for the LORD,
and he stooped toward me and heard my cry.
And he put a new song into my mouth,
a hymn to our God. **R.**

Sacrifice or offering you wished not,
but ears open to obedience you gave me.
Holocausts or sin-offerings you sought not;
then said I, "Behold I come." **R.**

"In the written scroll it is prescribed for me,
to do your will, O my God, is my delight,
and your law is within my heart!" **R.**

I announced your justice in the vast assembly;
I did not restrain my lips, as you, O LORD, know. **R.**

Second Reading
1 Corinthians 1:1–3

Paul, called to be an apostle of Christ Jesus by the will of God,
and Sosthenes our brother,
to the church of God that is in Corinth,
to you who have been sanctified in Christ Jesus, called to be holy,
with all those everywhere who call upon the name of
our Lord Jesus Christ, their Lord and ours.
Grace to you and peace from God our Father
and the Lord Jesus Christ.

Gospel
John 1:29–34

John the Baptist saw Jesus coming toward him and said,
"Behold, the Lamb of God, who takes away the sin of the world.
He is the one of whom I said,
'A man is coming after me who ranks ahead of me
because he existed before me.'
I did not know him,
but the reason why I came baptizing with water
was that he might be made known to Israel."
John testified further, saying,
"I saw the Spirit come down like a dove from heaven
and remain upon him.
I did not know him,
but the one who sent me to baptize with water told me,
'On whomever you see the Spirit come down and remain,
he is the one who will baptize with the Holy Spirit.'
Now I have seen and testified that he is the Son of God."

Here Am I, Lord; I Come to Do Your Will

HOMILY GIVEN ON JANUARY 19, 2020

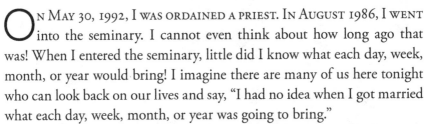

On May 30, 1992, I was ordained a priest. In August 1986, I went into the seminary. I cannot even think about how long ago that was! When I entered the seminary, little did I know what each day, week, month, or year would bring! I imagine there are many of us here tonight who can look back on our lives and say, "I had no idea when I got married what each day, week, month, or year was going to bring."

When I was in high school, I also had no idea what each day, week, month, or year would bring. We can reminisce about this no matter how old or young we are. The verse in the response to our psalm today is what was written on my ordination invitation, "Here am I, Lord; I come to do Your will." So many years ago, I had no idea what that was going to be. What was it going to mean to do God's will?

As we hear those words tonight, we have no idea what that is going to mean for each one of us—tonight, tomorrow, next week, or next year. But what if we started today, trying every day, to say, "Here I am, Lord" and stop right there? What a great image that is! The Lord is right there! Do we say, "Here I am, Lord? I am placing myself right here before you"? What peace that could bring! What contentment that could supply! What strength that could furnish! "Here I am, Lord; I come to do Your will."

Of course, that is difficult because we do not know what His will is. Maybe we are trying to figure out what His will is for us, what we are supposed to do with our life. Maybe we are trying to figure out what to do in a specific situation. If we are just trying to figure out what we want to have for dinner tonight, I guess God does care what we have for dinner, but not as much as what we are going to do with our lives. **We need to place ourselves in His presence and say, "Here I am, Lord." And further, take the chance to say, "I come to do Your will." Then God will guide us wherever we are supposed to go.**

The psalm says, "I have waited, waited for the LORD." We all have waited in one way or another, and we probably all waited for the Lord and thought, *Okay, any day now, you can do it.* I wonder how we wait when we wait for the Lord. Do we wait impatiently? Do we wait with anger? Do we wait with angst, or do we wait just peacefully saying, "Okay, Lord, in Your time, in Your way?" The psalm continues with an even more wonderful image, "and He stooped toward me and heard my cry." He stooped toward me, which means God is not waiting for us to come up to Him. He cares so much that He stooped toward us and then heard us. Maybe that is an image we can hold in our hearts and our minds when we think God is not listening.

We can say, "Lord, help me to believe that You are stooping down toward me. That You are here. That You are paying attention." The psalm goes further, "And He put a new song into my mouth." The Lord wants to place into our mouths things He wants us to say. The Lord then wants to place into our hearts how He wants us to live. He is not going to force-feed us. He is not going to force anything into our mouth. He is not going to force anything into our hearts either.

Tonight, may we ask for the grace to let Him in, to let Him place His words in our mouths, and to let Him place His will in our hearts. The psalm said, "but ears open to obedience You gave me." Ears open to obedience? We do not like to obey, but if there is anyone we should strive to obey, it would be God. I must open my ears. I must open my heart. I have to say, "Okay, Lord, what is Your will? Where do You want me to go?" And then the response, "and then said I, 'Behold, I come.'" What does that mean when we come to the Lord? "Behold, Lord, I come. Here I am, Lord. I come to You. I do not know where You are going to take me.

I do not know where You are going to lead me. I do not know what You are going to ask of me. But here I am. I come."

The second reading is a little strange in that it really doesn't say anything except, "Hello. How are you, my dear brothers and sisters?" That is all it really says. It does not really say anything else. But how does Paul say it, "Grace to you and peace from God, our Father and the Lord, Jesus Christ"?

How many times do we say to somebody, "How are you?" and we really do not care? Or we say, "How are you?" and really want a short answer. We do not want a long dissertation. How many times do we say, "How are you?" because we know that someone is struggling and something is going on? What if every time we greet somebody, we greeted them as Paul did in the reading tonight with Christ in our hearts? **What if every time we said, "How are you?" to somebody, we said it trying to remember Christ is within us? What if we did that the next time we had to greet somebody that we find difficult to greet, difficult to be with? We greet them remembering that Christ is within us.**

The gospel advises, "Behold the Lamb of God who takes away the sin of the world." We hear that phrase at the end of every Mass before Communion, "Lamb of God, You take away the sin of the world, have mercy on us ... have mercy on us ... grant us peace." We pray "Lamb of God," not Lion of God, but "Lamb of God," our Gentle Savior. The Jewish people, before they would sacrifice a lamb, would lay their hands on the lamb to pass onto that lamb all their sinfulness. Then they would sacrifice that lamb and believe that their sins would go up to God. That is what Jesus did. He sacrificed Himself as the Lamb of God. He wants to be the Lamb of God in our lives. He wants to be our Gentle Shepherd. John the Baptist said, "I did not know Him." He knew Jesus was his cousin, but he really did not know who He was until God revealed it to him.

How deeply do we want to know the Lord? Knowing the Lord is going to influence how we live our lives. If I am happy just to sort of know the Lord, I will live one way. If I really want to know the Lord, I am going to live a different way. How well do we want the Lord to know us? If we want Him to really know us, we are going to live one way. If we want to be a little more careful, we are going to live another way.

The first reading talked about the servant, "You are my servant." What does it mean to be a servant? It may mean we are trying to help somebody. Are we serving the Lord in the minimum way possible? Or are we striving to serve the Lord in the maximum way possible? **The Lord says that He does not want us to serve just Him. He wants us to be His light, and He wants us to spread that light. If this room, this church, was dark and we had just one light to use, it would help, but if all of us had a light, it would be wonderful and incredibly helpful. We are called to serve the Lord ourselves but also as part of a community we serve the Lord, and when we serve the Lord as a community, His light will shine!**

"HERE I AM, LORD; I COME TO DO YOUR WILL." These are challenging words, but maybe, each day, we can take the chance. "HERE I AM, LORD. YOU ARE MY LORD. I COME TO DO YOUR WILL."

READINGS FOR JANUARY 26, 2020

First Reading
Isaiah 8:23, 9:3
First the LORD degraded the land of Zebulun
and the land of Naphtali;
but in the end he has glorified the seaward road,
the land west of the Jordan,
the District of the Gentiles.
Anguish has taken wing, dispelled is darkness:
for there is no gloom where but now there was distress.
The people who walked in darkness
have seen a great light;
upon those who dwelt in the land of gloom
a light has shone.
You have brought them abundant joy
and great rejoicing,
as they rejoice before you as at the harvest,
as people make merry when dividing spoils.
For the yoke that burdened them,
the pole on their shoulder,
and the rod of their taskmaster
you have smashed, as on the day of Midian.

Responsorial Psalm
Psalm 27:1, 4, 13–14
R. The Lord is my light and my salvation.
The LORD is my light and my salvation;
whom should I fear?
The LORD is my life's refuge;
of whom should I be afraid? **R.**

One thing I ask of the LORD;
this I seek:
to dwell in the house of the LORD
all the days of my life,

that I may gaze on the loveliness of the LORD
and contemplate his temple. **R.**

I believe that I shall see the bounty of the LORD
in the land of the living.
Wait for the LORD with courage;
be stouthearted, and wait for the LORD. **R.**

Second Reading
1 Corinthians 1:10–13, 17

I urge you, brothers and sisters, in the name of our Lord Jesus Christ,
that all of you agree in what you say,
and that there be no divisions among you,
but that you be united in the same mind and in the same purpose.
For it has been reported to me about you, my brothers and sisters,
by Chloe's people, that there are rivalries among you.
I mean that each of you is saying,
"I belong to Paul," or "I belong to Apollos,"
or "I belong to Cephas," or "I belong to Christ."
Is Christ divided?
Was Paul crucified for you?
Or were you baptized in the name of Paul?
For Christ did not send me to baptize but to preach the gospel,
and not with the wisdom of human eloquence,
so that the cross of Christ might not be emptied of its meaning.

Gospel
Matthew 4:12–23

When Jesus heard that John had been arrested,
he withdrew to Galilee.
He left Nazareth and went to live in Capernaum by the sea,
in the region of Zebulun and Naphtali,
that what had been said through Isaiah the prophet
might be fulfilled:
Land of Zebulun and land of Naphtali,
the way to the sea, beyond the Jordan,

Galilee of the Gentiles,
the people who sit in darkness have seen a great light,
on those dwelling in a land overshadowed by death
light has arisen.
From that time on, Jesus began to preach and say,
"Repent, for the kingdom of heaven is at hand."
As he was walking by the Sea of Galilee, he saw two brothers,
Simon who is called Peter, and his brother Andrew,
casting a net into the sea; they were fishermen.
He said to them,
"Come after me, and I will make you fishers of men."
At once they left their nets and followed him.
He walked along from there and saw two other brothers,
James, the son of Zebedee, and his brother John.
They were in a boat, with their father Zebedee, mending their nets.
He called them, and immediately they left their boat and their father
and followed him.
He went around all of Galilee,
teaching in their synagogues, proclaiming the gospel of the kingdom,
and curing every disease and illness among the people.

The Road Less Traveled

HOMILY GIVEN ON JANUARY 26, 2020

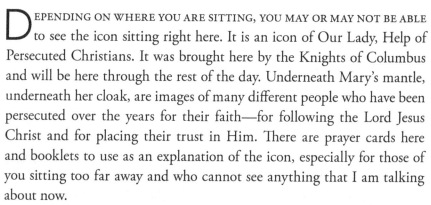

Depending on where you are sitting, you may or may not be able to see the icon sitting right here. It is an icon of Our Lady, Help of Persecuted Christians. It was brought here by the Knights of Columbus and will be here through the rest of the day. Underneath Mary's mantle, underneath her cloak, are images of many different people who have been persecuted over the years for their faith—for following the Lord Jesus Christ and for placing their trust in Him. There are prayer cards here and booklets to use as an explanation of the icon, especially for those of you sitting too far away and who cannot see anything that I am talking about now.

On Friday, there was a March for Life that acknowledged, in a real sense, that the unborn have the potential to be persecuted Christians. In our lives each time we listen to the Lord, the potential is there for us to be persecuted Christians because sometimes following the Lord means you take "a road less traveled."

You may need to go on a road with little or no support from others. As an example, there may be times we look at the things that are going on in social media and other media forms and say, "Wait a minute. This isn't good." In saying so, we have the potential to be persecuted Christians. There also may be times we look at all that is going on around us and say, "Well, it doesn't matter. It is not a big deal. It's not really hurting anybody." However, if we truly try to listen to the Lord, we might need to look at all the different things happening around us and ask, "Is this healthy and good for us?"

The other night, I was flicking through the channels, and I will not say what show or channel I was on, but I was amazed, not particularly by the language as much as the topic being discussed! I then wondered how many times I may have just looked at some inappropriate show for a few minutes without even thinking and then realized it was wrong. But I may have also thought for those few minutes it was not a big deal and I was not really hurting anybody. We also sometimes laugh at inappropriate jokes, and it made me stop and think, *What are our children being exposed to today that we do not even think about? What do we want our children to see? What influences do we want them to have in their lives?*

The readings today speak about eternal life and the afterlife—what is to come as well as the here and now. Each of us in our own way must decide, "Am I willing to try to follow the Lord in my life, even if it means I may be persecuted? If I am willing to follow the ways of the Lord, will I ask myself how to monitor what my child is doing? Would I also be willing to stop my child when he/she is viewing something inappropriate? Will I be persecuted but still maintain my stance of knowing the difference between right and wrong?"

The first reading says, "Anguish has taken wing, dispelled is darkness: for there is no gloom where but now there was distress." In life, we may experience anguish, gloom, or darkness, but we can also experience God's light, right here, right now. If we choose to allow Him to be a part of all that we are, then we too become "the people who have walked in darkness, have seen a great light." Do we want to see the great light, which is the Lord Jesus Christ, or do we prefer to be in darkness? We are told, "You have brought them abundant joy and great rejoicing ... for the yoke that burdened them, the pole on their shoulder and the rod of their taskmaster, you have smashed."

The Lord wants us to allow Him to help to carry our burdens with us and for us. The Lord wants to give us the grace and strength we need to follow Him in our lives, even if it means we may be persecuted. "The Lord is my Light and my Salvation, whom should I fear, of whom should I be afraid?" If somehow each day we can let the Lord be our light, then no matter what comes at us, no matter where He might be asking us to walk, where other people may not want to walk, we can then do so without fear. And if we do become afraid, we can continue to walk anyway. We will know that Christ is with us. "One thing I ask of the Lord; this I seek: to dwell in the house of the Lord all the days of my life …"

In the end, this is what we all want as people of faith. We gather here today because one day we want to dwell in the house of the Lord, but here we are right now, in the house of the Lord. In this house, **He offers us His grace and strength to listen to Him and to follow Him, even when it might mean that we will be persecuted.**

St. Paul reminds us, "that there be no divisions among you, but that you be united in the same mind and in the same purpose." We can strive for that and start by being united with how Jesus wants us to live our lives. Paul reminds us that we all belong to Christ. So many times, we can get caught up in belonging to this world, even when we know that we all belong to Christ. If we belong to Him, we need to accept that we may still have some difficult moments in our lives, but His light is always there.

In the gospel, He reminded them to "Come after Me." Every day we can choose whether we are going to follow Him, and if we do so, it may mean persecution. I would like to read the prayer card that is here as I close this homily. The prayer that is written is, **"Oh God of all the nations, the one God who is and was and always will be. In Your providence, You will that Your Church be united to the suffering of Your Son. Look with mercy on Your servants who are persecuted for their faith in You. Grant them perseverance and courage to be worthy imitators of Christ. Bring Your wisdom upon leaders of nations to work for peace among all peoples. May Your Spirit open conversion for those who contradict Your will, so that we may live in harmony. Give us the grace to be united in truth and freedom and to always seek Your will in our lives, even if it means persecution."**

READINGS FOR FEBRUARY 2, 2020

First Reading
Malachi 3:1–4
Thus says the Lord GOD:
Lo, I am sending my messenger
to prepare the way before me;
and suddenly there will come to the temple
the LORD whom you seek,
and the messenger of the covenant whom you desire.
Yes, he is coming, says the LORD of hosts.
But who will endure the day of his coming?
And who can stand when he appears?
For he is like the refiner's fire,
or like the fuller's lye.
He will sit refining and purifying silver,
and he will purify the sons of Levi,
refining them like gold or like silver
that they may offer due sacrifice to the LORD.
Then the sacrifice of Judah and Jerusalem
will please the LORD,
as in the days of old, as in years gone by.

Responsorial Psalm
Psalms 24:7–10
R. Who is this king of glory? It is the Lord!
Lift up, O gates, your lintels;
reach up, you ancient portals,
that the king of glory may come in! **R.**

Who is this king of glory?
The LORD, strong and mighty,
the LORD, mighty in battle. **R.**

Lift up, O gates, your lintels;
reach up, you ancient portals,
that the king of glory may come in! **R.**

Who is this king of glory?
The LORD of hosts; he is the king of glory. **R.**

Second Reading
Hebrews 2:14–18
Since the children share in blood and flesh,
Jesus likewise shared in them,
that through death he might destroy the one
who has the power of death, that is, the devil,
and free those who through fear of death
had been subject to slavery all their life.
Surely he did not help angels
but rather the descendants of Abraham;
therefore, he had to become like his brothers and sisters
in every way,
that he might be a merciful and faithful high priest before God
to expiate the sins of the people.
Because he himself was tested through what he suffered,
he is able to help those who are being tested.

Gospel
Luke 2:22–40
When the days were completed for their purification
according to the law of Moses,
Mary and Joseph took Jesus up to Jerusalem
to present him to the Lord,
just as it is written in the law of the Lord,
Every male that opens the womb shall be consecrated to the Lord,
and to offer the sacrifice of
a pair of turtledoves or two young pigeons,
in accordance with the dictate in the law of the Lord.
Now there was a man in Jerusalem whose name was Simeon.
This man was righteous and devout,
awaiting the consolation of Israel,
and the Holy Spirit was upon him.
It had been revealed to him by the Holy Spirit

that he should not see death
before he had seen the Christ of the Lord.
He came in the Spirit into the temple;
and when the parents brought in the child Jesus
to perform the custom of the law in regard to him,
he took him into his arms and blessed God, saying:
"Now, Master, you may let your servant go
in peace, according to your word,
for my eyes have seen your salvation,
which you prepared in sight of all the peoples,
a light for revelation to the Gentiles,
and glory for your people Israel."
The child's father and mother were amazed at what was said about him;
and Simeon blessed them and said to Mary his mother,
"Behold, this child is destined
for the fall and rise of many in Israel,
and to be a sign that will be contradicted
—and you yourself a sword will pierce—
so that the thoughts of many hearts may be revealed."
There was also a prophetess, Anna,
the daughter of Phanuel, of the tribe of Asher.
She was advanced in years,
having lived seven years with her husband after her marriage,
and then as a widow until she was eighty-four.
She never left the temple,
but worshiped night and day with fasting and prayer.
And coming forward at that very time,
she gave thanks to God and spoke about the child
to all who were awaiting the redemption of Jerusalem.
When they had fulfilled all the prescriptions
of the law of the Lord,
they returned to Galilee, to their own town of Nazareth.
The child grew and became strong, filled with wisdom;
and the favor of God was upon him.

Beware of the Packaging!

HOMILY GIVEN ON FEBRUARY 2, 2020

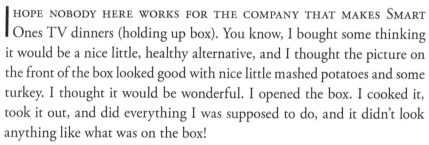

I HOPE NOBODY HERE WORKS FOR THE COMPANY THAT MAKES Smart Ones TV dinners (holding up box). You know, I bought some thinking it would be a nice little, healthy alternative, and I thought the picture on the front of the box looked good with nice little mashed potatoes and some turkey. I thought it would be wonderful. I opened the box. I cooked it, took it out, and did everything I was supposed to do, and it didn't look anything like what was on the box!

I thought to myself, *The reason I bought this is because of the packaging. On the outside, it looked really good, but on the inside, it wasn't as good as I had hoped it would be.*

That's the nature of sin, if we stop and think about it. There are a lot of things in life that look good on the outside. They look like they're going to make us happy, solve all our problems, and bring us joy and they're not going to hurt anybody. However, on the inside, they're not quite as good as they seemed to be on the outside.

What about ourselves? We can look one way on the outside—all of us sometimes put on a façade—but what is going on in the inside? And for many of us, if not all of us, sometimes the inside does not match the outside. Today we celebrate the Feast of the Presentation of the Lord. **The Lord was presented in the temple, and the Lord, in a very real sense, wants to present Himself to us each day. He wants to be part of what's going on inside so there's a better chance that the outside**

actually matches what's going on inside. You know, you buy these meals with the nice picture on the outside, but when opened, it's not like it was represented in that picture!

At times, we can even think that's the way it is with God. "On the outside, God, You look like You are loving and caring and You are going to take care of everything, but on the inside, it doesn't seem to be that way." However, **God is the same inside and out. What we're told God is, God is. It's just a matter of whether we're going to allow God to come inside of us or not, as God is!**

A few days ago, I took a nice little hike with my dog, Maggie. We got to this one spot, and I looked up and thought, *Oh my goodness*. It was this big hill with many large rocks and other obstacles. I just stood there for a minute. Of course, my dog just ran right up and stood there, looking at me thinking, *Why don't you come?*

And I still wasn't sure if I could make it or not. However, I started up, and eventually I got a little closer. But then the dog got sick of waiting for me. She came back down. She seemed to be saying, "Come on. Come on. I'll show you how to get there."

I am watching her and thinking, *So now you're going to do it twice, and I can't even do it once!* By the time I got to the top, I felt a little better. I thought to myself, *Okay. I accomplished that.*

In our lives, oftentimes it can feel as if we're trying to climb a hill. We stand at the bottom of the hill and think, *I don't know if I can get up there or not.* In those moments of trial, in those moments of difficulty, we discover God is our foundation, our strength. If we choose, we can draw closer to the Lord.

The first reading said, "The Lord, whom you seek and the messenger of the covenant, whom you desire." Who do we seek? Who do we desire? Who is the God we are seeking? Is it a God that we want to create as what we suppose Him to be, or is it who God wants to be? "Refining them like gold or like silver" is what God wants to do. He wants to refine us. He wants to make us pure. He wants to help us to be a better person, but in order to do that, we need to let Him inside. We need to let Him be a part of us, and somehow we need to recognize, in the midst of our trials, our difficulties, if we embrace those moments, they can bring us closer to the Lord.

The psalm said, "Who is this King of Glory? It is the Lord!" Once we take the chance and let Him inside, then He can be our King of Glory. The psalm goes on to say, "the King of Glory may come in!" May come in! Our King, who was presented and whose feast we celebrate today, is the light that came into the world. He wants to come in, not just to the world, but into our hearts. The Lord, strong and mighty, the Lord mighty in battle, wants to come in. **What battles are we fighting in our lives that we're not letting the Lord into? What battles does the Lord want to be a part of in our lives and we're saying, "Lord, I can handle this myself"? What battles are happening in our lives because we're not handing things over to God? So in some sense, the battles exist because we create them**. How many times do we worry about things and get all caught up in issues and **God is saying, "Just give it to me. Just give it to me"?**

The second reading explains, "Since the children share in blood and flesh, Jesus, likewise, shared in them." That's what the feast day of the Presentation of the Lord, celebrated today, is all about. Jesus came into our world to share in our body and blood, to share in our flesh. This is the connection between Christmas, which was forty days ago, and now. At Christmas, when the Light came into the world, and now, when we celebrate that Light being presented to us, that Light that wants to come inside of us is the same Light that wants to become a part of us.

The reading said, "He wants to free those who through fear of death have been subject to slavery all their life." Fear can paralyze us, **but when we let the Lord in, He can set us free. He is able to help those being tested because He Himself was tested through what he suffered, that is, not those who were tested but those who are being tested right now. He didn't just help people two thousand years ago, but He wants to help us right now, in the midst of our testing, our trials.**

The gospel said that Mary and Joseph took Jesus up to Jerusalem to present Him to the Lord, and Simeon took Him into his arms. Imagine taking Jesus into your arms. And what does Simeon say, "Now, Master, You may let your servant go in peace, according to Your word for my eyes have seen Your salvation"?

At the end of our lives, wouldn't that be wonderful if we could say that to the Lord? "I have seen Your salvation. I have felt Your presence inside of me. Whenever You're ready, I'll go and be with You." It doesn't mean we're

Sunday Snippets from Fr. Dan

running to get into heaven, but we should be sitting here saying, "God, what a wonderful thing You offer! When I allow Your light inside of me, then You offer me the light of eternal life."

"Behold, this Child is destined for the fall and rise of many …" (Luke 2:34). When we let Him in, that doesn't mean there won't be difficulties. But when we let Him in, amazing things can happen! In the midst of our trials, we can choose to see those trials as terrible things, those hills we have to climb. But we can also see them as opportunities to grow closer to the Lord. When we find that the packaging doesn't quite meet what's inside, that's what sin is. We hope life is always going to be wonderful, but at times, we find out it's not. But that is okay. God's packaging does coincide with what is inside.

God is who He is. God wants to dwell deep within us. Will we allow Him in? Will we truly allow Him to be a part of everything we are? On this Feast of the Presentation of the Lord, will we allow Him to be our light?

READINGS FOR FEBRUARY 16, 2020

First Reading
Sirach 15:15–20

If you choose you can keep the commandments, they will save you;
if you trust in God, you too shall live;
he has set before you fire and water;
to whichever you choose, stretch forth your hand.
Before man are life and death, good and evil,
whichever he chooses shall be given him.
Immense is the wisdom of the LORD;
he is mighty in power, and all-seeing.
The eyes of God are on those who fear him;
he understands man's every deed.
No one does he command to act unjustly,
to none does he give license to sin.

Responsorial Psalm
Psalm 119:1–2, 4–5, 17–18, 33–34

R. Blessed are they who follow the law of the LORD!

Blessed are they whose way is blameless,
who walk in the law of the LORD.
Blessed are they who observe his decrees,
who seek him with all their heart. **R.**

You have commanded that your precepts
be diligently kept.
Oh, that I might be firm in the ways
of keeping your statutes! **R.**

Be good to your servant, that I may live
and keep your words.
Open my eyes, that I may consider
the wonders of your law. **R.**

Instruct me, O LORD, in the way of your statutes,
that I may exactly observe them.

Give me discernment, that I may observe your law
and keep it with all my heart. **R.**

Second Reading
1 Corinthians 2:6–10
Brothers and sisters:
We speak a wisdom to those who are mature,
not a wisdom of this age,
nor of the rulers of this age who are passing away.
Rather, we speak God's wisdom, mysterious, hidden,
which God predetermined before the ages for our glory,
and which none of the rulers of this age knew;
for, if they had known it,
they would not have crucified the Lord of glory.
But as it is written:
*What eye has not seen, and ear has not heard,
and what has not entered the human heart,
what God has prepared for those who love him,*
this God has revealed to us through the Spirit.
For the Spirit scrutinizes everything, even the depths of God.

Gospel
Matthew 5:17–37
Jesus said to his disciples:
"Do not think that I have come to abolish the law or the prophets.
I have come not to abolish but to fulfill.
Amen, I say to you, until heaven and earth pass away,
not the smallest letter or the smallest part of a letter
will pass from the law,
until all things have taken place.
Therefore, whoever breaks one of the least of these commandments
and teaches others to do so
will be called least in the kingdom of heaven.
But whoever obeys and teaches these commandments
will be called greatest in the kingdom of heaven.
I tell you, unless your righteousness surpasses

that of the scribes and Pharisees,
you will not enter the kingdom of heaven.
"You have heard that it was said to your ancestors,
You shall not kill; and whoever kills will be liable to judgment.
But I say to you,
whoever is angry with his brother
will be liable to judgment;
and whoever says to his brother, 'Raqa,'
will be answerable to the Sanhedrin;
and whoever says, 'You fool,'
will be liable to fiery Gehenna.
Therefore, if you bring your gift to the altar,
and there recall that your brother
has anything against you,
leave your gift there at the altar,
go first and be reconciled with your brother,
and then come and offer your gift.
Settle with your opponent quickly while on the way to court.
Otherwise your opponent will hand you over to the judge,
and the judge will hand you over to the guard,
and you will be thrown into prison.
Amen, I say to you,
you will not be released until you have paid the last penny.
"You have heard that it was said,
You shall not commit adultery.
But I say to you,
everyone who looks at a woman with lust
has already committed adultery with her in his heart.
If your right eye causes you to sin,
tear it out and throw it away.
It is better for you to lose one of your members
than to have your whole body thrown into Gehenna.
And if your right hand causes you to sin,
cut it off and throw it away.
It is better for you to lose one of your members
than to have your whole body go into Gehenna.

"It was also said,
Whoever divorces his wife must give her a bill of divorce.
But I say to you,
whoever divorces his wife—unless the marriage is unlawful—
causes her to commit adultery,
and whoever marries a divorced woman commits adultery.
"Again you have heard that it was said to your ancestors,
Do not take a false oath,
but make good to the Lord all that you vow.
But I say to you, do not swear at all;
not by heaven, for it is God's throne;
nor by the earth, for it is his footstool;
nor by Jerusalem, for it is the city of the great King.
Do not swear by your head,
for you cannot make a single hair white or black.
Let your 'Yes' mean 'Yes,' and your 'No' mean 'No.'
Anything more is from the evil one."

Pointed Toward the Lord

HOMILY GIVEN ON FEBRUARY 16, 2020

Last Sunday, a young girl in our parish gave me a box she had made for me. It is very well thought-out. It is a tissue box, and on the top are the three kings holding gold, frankincense, and myrrh. Mary and Jesus are kneeling, and they are kneeling to God. A little circle represents the sun, and the sun is also pointing toward God. The mother of this little girl told me that this all came out of her child's head. Her parents did not say anything to her about this before they were shown her creation.

"This was going on in our child's mind," they said.

I thought to myself how amazing it is that children can often share with us ideas that, for whatever reason, as we get older, we cannot come up with ourselves. This little girl had Mary, Jesus, and the three kings all praying and pointing toward God. Somehow, in our lives, if we could make sure that everything we do is always pointed toward God, things would be a little different. We would be reminded that God is everywhere and not just "up there" somewhere.

The other day, I had the opportunity to watch a movie on Amazon about two people in 1862 who went up in a hot-air balloon to exceed the then-present record of 23,000 feet. They actually went up to 37,000 feet and had all sorts of trouble but were able to eventually land. Everything worked out, but on the way up, the storms, cold temperature, and lack of oxygen almost killed them. Even so, they lived through it all!

When we go up to God, when we try to get closer to God, we think life will get easier, but the reality is that the closer we try to get to God, the more storms we may encounter, the more bad weather we may face, including that it may get colder and we may feel like we are lacking in oxygen. The closer we get to God, the more challenging it may be to look at our lives here. The closer we get to God, we may feel that life is more difficult and it does not always make sense. Even so, we can choose to strive to grow closer to God, knowing it may mean more trials and tribulations. Or we can choose to stay far away from Him.

The readings today basically talk about the choices we make every day. We can choose to keep the commandments or not to follow what God wants us to do, to go another way and take a different path. It is early in the day right now, so we probably have not made too many choices yet. But as the day goes on, we are going to have plenty of opportunities to make a choice whether we are going to stay pointed toward God, as in the box the little girl made. **This box models for us the direction in which we can make our choices; we can move toward God or in a different direction.**

"He has set before you fire and water." Water refreshes. The Lord wants to refresh us. Fire can burn us. Things that happen to our world can burn us, but the Lord wants to be there with us. Will we choose the eyes of God on us? **When we choose God, then we can remember that His eyes are always on us. That does not have to cause us fear but can give us great joy and hope since we know He is watching and paying attention. When we choose God, our eyes stay on Him.** Somehow, even unconsciously, if we can remember to keep our eyes on God, we never have to fear. **We still are responsible for our choices; He does not give us license to sin.**

Sometimes we may think that we can do whatever we want to do, if we feel what we are doing is not really hurting anybody. The reading reminds us that God did not give us license to sin. He did not want us to do whatever we wanted, even if the only person being hurt is ourselves. When we choose to put God and His commandments aside, it is a lot easier to do whatever we want to do. When we choose to point our lives toward God, it is a little more difficult. **"Blessed are they who follow the law of the Lord! Blessed are they whose way is blameless, who walk in the**

law of the Lord. Blessed are they who observe His decrees, who seek Him with all their heart."

The second reading said, "Rather, we speak God's wisdom, mysterious, hidden …" God's wisdom is mysterious, and it would be wonderful if we could live our lives with His wisdom. Now, we might not be able to do that, but we can certainly choose to live our lives in a way that allows His wisdom to work through us and be a part of us. God, who has revealed to us through the Spirit, wants His Spirit to dwell within us. He wants His Spirit to be a part of everything we are. He is not going to force us. He wants us to choose. It would be convenient if we could just choose once and done, but we choose every day. Some days, we choose five, ten, or fifteen times whether we will follow God's will!

In the gospel today, Jesus mentions a lot of ideas on a lot of different things, and we could spend a lot of time on each one of them. "I have come not to abolish but to fulfill … Therefore, whoever breaks one of the least of these Commandments, teaches others to do so and will be called least in the kingdom of heaven." What Jesus is reminding us is that in all our choices, we should remember Him. Choose Him; choose to follow Him so others too can follow Him. "You shall not kill; but I say to you, whoever kills is liable to judgment." Jesus is also saying that whoever is angry with his brother is liable to judgment. Sometimes, we think the fifth commandment just says to us, **"Well, I haven't killed anybody," but when we hold on to anger, when we hold on to resentment, it slowly kills us inside. If we choose to follow the Lord, then we are going to be able to let it go. If this seems impossible, maybe the one with whom we are really angry is God because something is not or did not happen the way we wanted it to occur. The lesson is that when we point ourselves toward God, He can help us heal despite the anger we may be feeling.**

God tells us not to commit adultery, but if we look at somebody with lust, the sin has already been committed. The question is, "What do we see, watch, or prefer in music? Are these things God would want us to choose?" We need to be sure that "yes means yes" and our "no means no." We pray today that we will stay pointed toward the Lord in all we do so we are honest in replying yes or no!

The little girl and her box show us how important it is to stay pointed toward God and that we should strive to move higher and higher toward Him. Yes, we may encounter difficulties. Most likely, our journey will get harder, not easier, but we can always make a choice in the right direction. Every day we can choose to be facing toward or away from Him. Starting today, we need to choose Him in all we say and do and in all the decisions we make. **Let us try to allow the Lord to be part of our lives always and in all ways. Choose God each day!**

READINGS FOR MARCH 1, 2020

First Reading
Genesis 2:7–9; 3:1–7

The LORD God formed man out of the clay of the ground
and blew into his nostrils the breath of life,
and so man became a living being.
Then the LORD God planted a garden in Eden, in the east,
and placed there the man whom he had formed.
Out of the ground the LORD God made various trees grow
that were delightful to look at and good for food,
with the tree of life in the middle of the garden
and the tree of the knowledge of good and evil.
Now the serpent was the most cunning of all the animals
that the LORD God had made.
The serpent asked the woman,
"Did God really tell you not to eat
from any of the trees in the garden?"
The woman answered the serpent:
"We may eat of the fruit of the trees in the garden;
it is only about the fruit of the tree
in the middle of the garden that God said,
'You shall not eat it or even touch it, lest you die.'"
But the serpent said to the woman:
"You certainly will not die!
No, God knows well that the moment you eat of it
your eyes will be opened and you will be like gods
who know what is good and what is evil."
The woman saw that the tree was good for food,
pleasing to the eyes, and desirable for gaining wisdom.
So she took some of its fruit and ate it;
and she also gave some to her husband, who was with her,
and he ate it.
Then the eyes of both of them were opened,
and they realized that they were naked;
so they sewed fig leaves together
and made loincloths for themselves.

Responsorial Psalm
Psalm 51:3–6, 12–13, 17
R. Be merciful, O Lord, for we have sinned.
Have mercy on me, O God, in your goodness;
in the greatness of your compassion wipe out my offense.
Thoroughly wash me from my guilt
and of my sin cleanse me. **R.**

For I acknowledge my offense,
and my sin is before me always:
"Against you only have I sinned,
and done what is evil in your sight." **R.**

A clean heart create for me, O God,
and a steadfast spirit renew within me.
Cast me not out from your presence,
and your Holy Spirit take not from me. **R.**

Give me back the joy of your salvation,
and a willing spirit sustain in me.
O Lord, open my lips,
and my mouth shall proclaim your praise. **R.**

Second Reading
Romans 5:12–19
Brothers and sisters:
Through one man sin entered the world,
and through sin, death,
and thus death came to all men, inasmuch as all sinned—
for up to the time of the law, sin was in the world,
though sin is not accounted when there is no law.
But death reigned from Adam to Moses,
even over those who did not sin
after the pattern of the trespass of Adam,
who is the type of the one who was to come.

But the gift is not like the transgression.
For if by the transgression of the one, the many died,
how much more did the grace of God
and the gracious gift of the one man Jesus Christ
overflow for the many.
And the gift is not like the result of the one who sinned.
For after one sin there was the judgment that brought condemnation;
but the gift, after many transgressions, brought acquittal.
For if, by the transgression of the one,
death came to reign through that one,
how much more will those who receive the abundance of grace
and of the gift of justification
come to reign in life through the one Jesus Christ.
In conclusion, just as through one transgression
condemnation came upon all,
so, through one righteous act,
acquittal and life came to all.
For just as through the disobedience of the one man
the many were made sinners,
so, through the obedience of the one,
the many will be made righteous.

Gospel
Matthew 4:1–11
At that time Jesus was led by the Spirit into the desert
to be tempted by the devil.
He fasted for forty days and forty nights,
and afterwards he was hungry.
The tempter approached and said to him,
"If you are the Son of God,
command that these stones become loaves of bread."
He said in reply,
"It is written:
One does not live on bread alone,
but on every word that comes forth
from the mouth of God."

Then the devil took him to the holy city,
and made him stand on the parapet of the temple,
and said to him, "If you are the Son of God, throw yourself down.
For it is written:
He will command his angels concerning you
and with their hands they will support you,
lest you dash your foot against a stone."
Jesus answered him,
"Again it is written,
You shall not put the Lord, your God, to the test."
Then the devil took him up to a very high mountain,
and showed him all the kingdoms of the world in their magnificence,
and he said to him, "All these I shall give to you,
if you will prostrate yourself and worship me."
At this, Jesus said to him,
"Get away, Satan!
It is written:
The Lord, your God, shall you worship
and him alone shall you serve."
Then the devil left him and, behold,
angels came and ministered to him.

Invite the Lord In

HOMILY GIVEN ON MARCH 1, 2020

The other day I was sitting in the sanctuary at Mass, and my mind started wandering—it's really bad if the priest's mind starts wandering a little bit! But my mind started wandering, and I was looking at all the different shades of purple there on display, the shades of purple on my vestment and the different shades of purple on the two banners, for example. That prompted me to think of all the different types of people there are and all the different ways God has created us.

Then I thought of the readings today that talk about temptations and all the different ways that we are tempted. Some of us may be tempted in the same way as others. But even the way those temptations happen is different, as is the depth of those temptations, and the difficulties we may face when it comes to certain temptations. The first line in the gospel says, "Jesus was led by the Spirit into the desert to be tempted by the devil."

Now that doesn't make a lot of sense. Why would the Spirit lead Jesus into the desert knowing he was going to be tempted? Perhaps what was meant is that the Spirit was there with Jesus as he went to face His temptations. Maybe that's something each and every one of us can embrace, **that whatever temptations we face, the Spirit is there with us, and we're not alone.**

Sometimes, when we choose to put blinders on and don't want to see God, we don't want to see the Spirit there. But temptation is too strong, and we forget that God is there! He fasted for forty days and forty nights, and afterward he was hungry. He was so hungry that he was ripe for temptation. If we were that hungry, I wonder if we'd be able to resist temptations. Perhaps there's times in our lives where we feel we're in such distress that we can't resist the temptation. **That's when we ask God to help us to remember that He is always there.** He is there in the midst of every temptation, and He wants to enter into that temptation and be a part of us.

Then we have the temptations that Jesus faced. Perhaps the difference with Jesus is that He faced those temptations, not looking at the short term, but the long term. Sometimes the reason we are led into whatever temptations, which then lead us to sin, is because we are just focused on the short term. We just focus on the moment. If we can focus beyond the moment, if we could somehow step back and ask, "How am I going to feel an hour, a month, or a year from now?" or whatever the time frame, then we might just be able to face those temptations differently.

"All these I shall give to You if you will prostrate Yourself and worship me." And what does Jesus say? "Get away Satan!" And we can do the same thing. We could say, "Get away, Satan! Jesus be with me." "The Lord your God shall you worship and Him alone shall you serve." That's a good opportunity for us to say, "Who do I worship? What do I worship? If I worship God, do I then call upon Him and trust the strength that only He can give?"

The second reading said, "For just as through the disobedience of the one man, the many were made sinners, so through the obedience of the One, the many will be made righteous." Look at the obedience of the One, the Lord Jesus Christ, who was willing to suffer and die for us so we could have eternal life. **Jesus is the reason for hope; Lent is really a season of hope**, the season where we remember that God's mercy, love, forgiveness, and strength exists. That's why we're here. **We're here tonight because somewhere, inside of ourselves, we recognize that we need God's love, mercy, strength, and hope.**

The psalm says, "Be merciful, O Lord, for we have sinned." But it doesn't stop there. The Lord wants to show us His mercy. One of the ways He does that is in the Sacrament of Reconciliation. In this sacrament, we can feel the words of this psalm, "Thoroughly wash me of my guilt and of my sin cleanse me." Yes, we can go by ourselves to the Lord and ask for forgiveness, and yes, He wants to cleanse us. But the Sacrament of Reconciliation gives us a greater opportunity to feel that forgiveness and that mercy, to hear somebody say to us, "You are forgiven." "A clean heart create for me, O God, and a steadfast spirit renew within me." Do we truly want God to create a clean heart within us? For if we do, then things are different. "Give me back the joy of your salvation and a willing spirit sustain in me," **a willing spirit.**

Then we hear the reading in Genesis, "Now the serpent was the most cunning of all the animals that the Lord God had made." That's the thing with temptation. Temptation can be very cunning. **Temptations make us think that they're the best thing and that they're going to make us very happy. The problem is temptations only make us happy for a short while.** Adam and Eve learned that. "Did God really tell you not to eat from any of the trees in the Garden?" We could probably take that same question and make it applicable in our lives. "Did God really say that you should _____?" Fill in the blank with whatever temptation you may be facing.

After they sinned, they recognized that they were naked. Before they sinned, they were not aware of this. But God wants us to be naked before Him. He wants us to stand before Him and say, "Here I am, Lord," and then He wants to enter deep within and give us His grace and strength.

Yes, there are many different shades of purple. There are many different people. There are many different temptations we all face, and we all face them differently. However, the Spirit is there. The Spirit led Jesus into the desert, not so Jesus could be tempted, but so Jesus would know that He was not alone.

That same Spirit is there for us! We know in the midst of our temptations that we are not alone. May we take the chance to invite the Lord in during this Lenten season. May we strive to walk closer to the Lord!

READINGS FOR MARCH 8, 2020

First Reading
Genesis 12:1–4a
The LORD said to Abram:
"Go forth from the land of your kinsfolk
and from your father's house to a land that I will show you.
"I will make of you a great nation,
and I will bless you;
I will make your name great,
so that you will be a blessing.
I will bless those who bless you
and curse those who curse you.
All the communities of the earth
shall find blessing in you."
Abram went as the LORD directed him.

Responsorial Psalm
Psalm 33:4–5, 18–20, 22
R. Lord, let your mercy be on us, as we place our trust in you.
Upright is the word of the LORD,
and all his works are trustworthy.
He loves justice and right;
of the kindness of the LORD the earth is full. **R.**

See, the eyes of the LORD are upon those who fear him,
upon those who hope for his kindness,
to deliver them from death
and preserve them in spite of famine. **R.**

Our soul waits for the LORD,
who is our help and our shield.
May your kindness, O LORD, be upon us
who have put our hope in you. **R.**

Second Reading
2 Timothy 1:8b–10
Beloved:
Bear your share of hardship for the gospel
with the strength that comes from God.
He saved us and called us to a holy life,
not according to our works
but according to his own design
and the grace bestowed on us in Christ Jesus before time began,
but now made manifest
through the appearance of our savior Christ Jesus,
who destroyed death and brought life and immortality
to light through the gospel.

Gospel
Matthew 17:1–9
Jesus took Peter, James, and John his brother,
and led them up a high mountain by themselves.
And he was transfigured before them;
his face shone like the sun
and his clothes became white as light.
And behold, Moses and Elijah appeared to them,
conversing with him.
Then Peter said to Jesus in reply,
"Lord, it is good that we are here.
If you wish, I will make three tents here,
one for you, one for Moses, and one for Elijah."
While he was still speaking, behold,
a bright cloud cast a shadow over them,
then from the cloud came a voice that said,
"This is my beloved Son, with whom I am well pleased;
listen to him."
When the disciples heard this, they fell prostrate
and were very much afraid.
But Jesus came and touched them, saying,
"Rise, and do not be afraid."

And when the disciples raised their eyes,
they saw no one else but Jesus alone.
As they were coming down from the mountain,
Jesus charged them,
"Do not tell the vision to anyone
until the Son of Man has been raised from the dead."

Still and Quiet with the Lord

HOMILY GIVEN ON MARCH 8, 2020

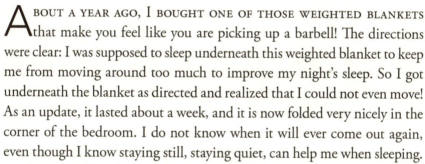

About a year ago, I bought one of those weighted blankets that make you feel like you are picking up a barbell! The directions were clear: I was supposed to sleep underneath this weighted blanket to keep me from moving around too much to improve my night's sleep. So I got underneath the blanket as directed and realized that I could not even move! As an update, it lasted about a week, and it is now folded very nicely in the corner of the bedroom. I do not know when it will ever come out again, even though I know staying still, staying quiet, can help me when sleeping.

Staying still and staying quiet can also help us in life. The psalm said, "Lord, let Your mercy be on us." What if we pictured the Lord's mercy being on us, just like one of those weighted blankets? We could be still and quiet in His presence. For many of us, it is difficult to be still and quiet. If we can imagine that the Lord is on us, we might be still and quiet with the Lord and grow in the ability to trust in the Lord.

The readings today are all about trust. We can get so busy, so involved with so many other things that it is difficult to trust. The psalm goes on to say, "Let Your mercy be on us, as we place our trust in You." Another image might be placing our trust in the Lord as if the Lord were a ghost sitting here in front of us and we could place our trust inside Him. What a wonderful image to place ourselves, our trust, inside the Lord and to trust that the Lord then places Himself inside us. All His trustworthy works would be inside us!

When we take the time to be still and to be quiet with the Lord, even at those moments when it is difficult to trust, we can find that we are able to do so. "Our soul waits for the Lord." Our souls are the very depth of who we are. So many times, we wait for the Lord, but we wait for the Lord on the surface. We wait for Him in our time, but to wait for the Lord in our souls means we are waiting for the Lord to go deep within us. It takes time for Him to go deep within us. It takes time for us to feel His presence deep within. That is why it is so important and so helpful to be still and quiet with the Lord.

Right now we can choose to be still and quiet with the Lord. Maybe today is the day. We can try ten seconds, then thirty seconds, and then a minute. Just remain still and quiet and let the Lord deep within our souls. Maybe right now we could take time to be still and quiet with the Lord. (Pause and reflect.)

During those times of being still and quiet, we can focus on the Lord going deep within our souls. It is then we can trust He is guiding us, He is leading us, and He genuinely wants to be a part of our lives and that we can truly feel we are not walking alone. There, in our souls, we can involve Him in all our choices and all our decisions. "Our soul waits for the Lord, who is our help and our shield."

The other day, someone pointed out to me that the words "I will" are used five times in the first reading. The Lord says, "I will make of you a great nation and I will bless you." The Lord is giving His support to Abram. And the Lord supports us in the same way in that He will always be there for us, He will walk with us, and He will not abandon us. He is there for us! The last line of the first reading said, "Abram went as the Lord directed him," even though Abram might have been unsure about why the Lord was asking him to do this. Abram may not have wanted to go, but ultimately he did not ask why. In our lives perhaps, there are many times we ask, "Why?" Maybe we get an answer; most often we do not. But do we go anyway?

In the second reading, we are called to just trust. We should "bear your share of hardship for the Gospel with the strength that comes from God." How can God give us His strength? When we sit quietly with Him and when we are still with Him, we will realize that He saved us and called us to a holy life. Lent is about change, about looking at ourselves and asking ourselves how we can become more holy. We need to ask the Lord to help us want to become more holy and to inquire, "Lord, where do I need to change?"

The gospel talks about Jesus's transfiguration. Jesus changed in appearance. **The Lord wants to change us, not just on the outside, but deep within.** Each of us needs to discover where God is asking us to change, where he is asking us to live our lives in a different way. "and His clothes became white as light." Wouldn't it be wonderful to be white as light, to have that purity in our lives? It is possible when we sit quietly with the Lord in stillness. **At the end of the gospel, we hear, "This is my beloved Son, with whom I am well pleased." May we strive to be pleasing to the Lord.**

Starting today, may we take the time to sit quietly with the Lord so we can listen to Him. We are told Jesus touched those who were afraid and said, "Rise and do not be afraid" (Matthew 17:7). The Lord says those same words to us today. So if we can picture one of those weighted blankets and put it on ourselves so we cannot move at all, then we can use that image to help us stop and be still and quiet with the Lord, even if it's only for ten seconds. **When we are still and quiet with the Lord, we can trust in His presence in our lives more fully.**

READINGS FOR MARCH 15, 2020

First Reading
Exodus 17:3–7

In those days, in their thirst for water,
the people grumbled against Moses,
saying, "Why did you ever make us leave Egypt?
Was it just to have us die here of thirst
with our children and our livestock?"
So Moses cried out to the LORD,
"What shall I do with this people?
A little more and they will stone me!"
The LORD answered Moses,
"Go over there in front of the people,
along with some of the elders of Israel,
holding in your hand, as you go,
the staff with which you struck the river.
I will be standing there in front of you on the rock in Horeb.
Strike the rock, and the water will flow from it
for the people to drink."
This Moses did, in the presence of the elders of Israel.
The place was called Massah and Meribah,
because the Israelites quarreled there
and tested the LORD, saying,
"Is the LORD in our midst or not?"

Responsorial Psalm
Psalm 95:1–2, 6–9

R. If today you hear his voice, harden not your hearts.

Come, let us sing joyfully to the LORD;
let us acclaim the Rock of our salvation.
Let us come into his presence with thanksgiving;
let us joyfully sing psalms to him. **R.**

Come, let us bow down in worship;
let us kneel before the LORD who made us.

For he is our God,
and we are the people he shepherds, the flock he guides. **R.**

Oh, that today you would hear his voice:
"Harden not your hearts as at Meribah,
as in the day of Massah in the desert.
Where your fathers tempted me;
they tested me though they had seen my works." **R.**

Second Reading

Romans 5:1–2, 5–8
Brothers and sisters:
Since we have been justified by faith,
we have peace with God through our Lord Jesus Christ,
through whom we have gained access by faith
to this grace in which we stand,
and we boast in hope of the glory of God.
And hope does not disappoint,
because the love of God has been poured out into our hearts
through the Holy Spirit who has been given to us.
For Christ, while we were still helpless,
died at the appointed time for the ungodly.
Indeed, only with difficulty does one die for a just person,
though perhaps for a good person one might even find courage to die.
But God proves his love for us
in that while we were still sinners Christ died for us.

Gospel

John 4:5–42
Jesus came to a town of Samaria called Sychar,
near the plot of land that Jacob had given to his son Joseph.
Jacob's well was there.
Jesus, tired from his journey, sat down there at the well.
It was about noon.
A woman of Samaria came to draw water.
Jesus said to her,

"Give me a drink."
His disciples had gone into the town to buy food.
The Samaritan woman said to him,
"How can you, a Jew, ask me, a Samaritan woman, for a drink?"
—For Jews use nothing in common with Samaritans.—
Jesus answered and said to her,
"If you knew the gift of God
and who is saying to you, 'Give me a drink,'
you would have asked him
and he would have given you living water."
The woman said to him,
"Sir, you do not even have a bucket and the cistern is deep;
where then can you get this living water?
Are you greater than our father Jacob,
who gave us this cistern and drank from it himself
with his children and his flocks?"
Jesus answered and said to her,
"Everyone who drinks this water will be thirsty again;
but whoever drinks the water I shall give will never thirst;
the water I shall give will become in him
a spring of water welling up to eternal life."
The woman said to him,
"Sir, give me this water, so that I may not be thirsty
or have to keep coming here to draw water."
Jesus said to her,
"Go call your husband and come back."
The woman answered and said to him,
"I do not have a husband."
Jesus answered her,
"You are right in saying, 'I do not have a husband.'
For you have had five husbands,
and the one you have now is not your husband.
What you have said is true."
The woman said to him,
"Sir, I can see that you are a prophet.
Our ancestors worshiped on this mountain;

but you people say that the place to worship is in Jerusalem."
Jesus said to her,
"Believe me, woman, the hour is coming
when you will worship the Father
neither on this mountain nor in Jerusalem.
You people worship what you do not understand;
we worship what we understand,
because salvation is from the Jews.
But the hour is coming, and is now here,
when true worshipers will worship the Father in Spirit and truth;
and indeed the Father seeks such people to worship him.
God is Spirit, and those who worship him
must worship in Spirit and truth."
The woman said to him,
"I know that the Messiah is coming, the one called the Christ;
when he comes, he will tell us everything."
Jesus said to her,
"I am he, the one speaking with you."
At that moment his disciples returned,
and were amazed that he was talking with a woman,
but still no one said, "What are you looking for?"
or "Why are you talking with her?"
The woman left her water jar
and went into the town and said to the people,
"Come see a man who told me everything I have done.
Could he possibly be the Christ?"
They went out of the town and came to him.
Meanwhile, the disciples urged him, "Rabbi, eat."
But he said to them,
"I have food to eat of which you do not know."
So the disciples said to one another,
"Could someone have brought him something to eat?"
Jesus said to them,
"My food is to do the will of the one who sent me
and to finish his work.
Do you not say, 'In four months the harvest will be here'?

I tell you, look up and see the fields ripe for the harvest.
The reaper is already receiving payment
and gathering crops for eternal life,
so that the sower and reaper can rejoice together.
For here the saying is verified that 'One sows and another reaps.'
I sent you to reap what you have not worked for;
others have done the work,
and you are sharing the fruits of their work."
Many of the Samaritans of that town began to believe in him
because of the word of the woman who testified,
"He told me everything I have done."
When the Samaritans came to him,
they invited him to stay with them;
and he stayed there two days.
Many more began to believe in him because of his word,
and they said to the woman,
"We no longer believe because of your word;
for we have heard for ourselves,
and we know that this is truly the savior of the world."

Standing in His Grace

HOMILY GIVEN ON MARCH 15, 2020

Some of you know I like cowboy boots, and you may have noticed that the cowboy boots I am wearing today are a little different. I have never worn these at Mass before last night. These are my rattlesnake ones. The reason I wore them is, with everything going on right now [reference to COVID pandemic], I think we all need a reason to smile. So I just looked down and said, "OK!" Now I do have an orange pair made of alligator, and they would have really made us smile, but I did not think it was appropriate to wear that pair!

Amid all the fear happening right now, along with all the concern, worry, and trials we are facing, I think all of us just need something to remind us to smile. Maybe something that can remind us to smile is that we are not alone. God is here. God is present. This is an opportunity for us to look inside ourselves and ask, "What do I hold important? What are the important things in my life?"

Perhaps, as we continue in this Lenten season, it's an opportunity to see this as a season where we are called to draw closer to the Lord, a chance for us to get some perspective and to ask God to give us the grace and strength to have Him be one of the most important things, if not *the* most important thing, in our lives. All that is happening right now is new for all of us. It is new territory. We do not know what the next day, week, month, or year is going to bring. **What we do know, however, is that God is there and that God is walking with us.**

In the first reading, taken from Exodus, the Jewish people were going into a new land, and the Israelites had no idea what was going to happen. They did not know what was going to happen the next hour, let alone the next week or month.

They grumbled to Moses about their thirst for water, "Why did you ever make us leave Egypt?" What are we thirsting for today? Maybe we are thirsting for understanding or a way to figure everything out. Perhaps we are grumbling, in a sense, against God, "Why did You ever allow this to happen? Why?"

Then Moses said, "What shall I do with these people?"

I wonder if God is wondering the same thing today about us (that is, these people). I think that if God could speak directly to our hearts, He would want us to trust that He is here for us. He would want us to know He is truly present.

The last line of the first reading is "Is the Lord in our midst or not?" Maybe we are asking that question also. "Are you here or not?" *He is here.* Throughout all of history, there have been many trials, difficulties, and times where people have asked the Lord, "Are you here?" And He was there, and He will be there for us. There is no reason to think He was there for the last thousands of years but He is not going to be here now! It is an opportunity for us to pause, reset, and ask God for the grace to hear His voice.

As the psalm says, **"If today you hear His voice, harden not your hearts."** In a sense, when we slow down, we have a better chance to hear His voice. The psalm continues, "He is the Rock of our salvation." **If somehow we can allow the Lord to be the Rock of our salvation, then no matter what comes down the pike, we will be OK.**

Today, we also asked God for the gift of perspective. The psalm goes on to say, "Come, let us bow down in worship; Let us kneel before the Lord who made us."

Last night, I was talking with one of our teenagers, and he said, "I don't know what I am going to do for the next two weeks."

If during the next few weeks and months we just spent a few extra moments kneeling before the Lord, bowing down before the Lord, it certainly could help us grow closer to Him. It certainly would help us gain perspective. God said, "They tested me though they had seen my works." We have seen God at work. We gather here today because there is something inside of us that says, "God is at work."

In the second reading, we see the words "faith," "hope," "peace," and "grace." "To this grace in which we stand." What a great image! Imagine standing in grace. There is a big bucket of grace sitting here, and we are standing in it. Here we go. We are going to get right into this bucket of grace. What a wonderful image! We can keep that image in our minds, the vision of standing in God's grace. It will be then that we will have faith, hope, and peace.

The gospel story is about the woman at the well. Jesus says, "Everyone who drinks this water will be thirsty again; but, whoever drinks the water I shall give, will never thirst; the water I shall give will become in him a spring of water welling up to eternal life."

The Lord Jesus Christ wants to be our nourishment, and He wants to feed us every day. All we must do is come to Him and stand in His grace. Jesus says to the woman, "Go call your husband and come back." She says, "I do not have a husband." Jesus says, "You are right in saying 'I do not have a husband.' For you have had five husbands."

She was looking for something or someone to bring her fulfillment in peace, something she could latch onto, and then she found Jesus. We are told in that gospel that she left her water jar and went to tell others about Him. That water jar was especially important, but she did not care. She left it there and just went and told everyone she met. She led other people to Jesus. We can lead other people to Jesus simply by trusting in Him.

So all of us need something to smile about with everything going on. I chose to wear my boots today. Maybe we can all think of something that can make us smile. **God is here. He is with us. He wants to be a part of our lives. May we not be afraid today and every day to stand in His grace!**